In Silent Moments

In Silent Moments

Thomas F. Walsh

CURRACH
PRESS

First published in 2007 by
CURRACH PRESS
55A Spruce Avenue, Stillorgan Industrial Park, Blackrock, Co. Dublin
www.currach.ie

1 3 5 4 2

A portion of the royalties from
this book will be donated to
Suzanne House, Tallaght.

Cover by Sin é Design
Origination by Currach Press
Printed by Betaprint, Bluebell Industrial Estate, Dublin 12
ISBN: 978 1 85607 953 2
The author has asserted his moral rights

For My Brothers and Sisters Whom I love

A Note to the Reader

A list of poems mentioned in the text is given on pp.
157-8.

Contents

Time Remembered

On 14 October 1992 our daughter, Caroline, died suddenly of meningococcal meningitis. She was sixteen years old.

My life is divided by that date; I count everything as being before or after. No parent ever recovers from such a catastrophe. Losing love, as the Paul Simon song says, is like a window in your heart. There remains a space which is never filled.

Caroline was a remarkable person. She loved laughter and living and she particularly loved the goodness that is in people. I know that her short life and death have inspired her friends and family. But for me, life, for a time, seemed to have no meaning. I could not go on without sensing 'the solving emptiness that lies just under all we do'. One of the ways by which I tried to cope was by writing. I have always been moved by poetry and the great authors of the past. I took refuge in 'Thoughts that do often lie too deep for tears'. I gathered poems that spoke to me from a half-forgotten childhood.

> And time remembered is grief forgotten,
> And frosts are slain and flowers begotten,
> And in green underwood and cover
> Blossom by blossom the spring begins.

And in time, the spring did, slowly, seem to appear. Things had not changed, but my perception of them had. To quote the words of the playwright Denis Potter from his final interview: 'Things are both more trivial than they ever were, and more important than they ever were, and the difference between the trivial and the important doesn't seem to matter. But the nowness of everything is absolutely wondrous.'

To try to understand life, you must come to terms with death and loss and heartbreak. To appreciate life, you have to savour the single moment of existence. The things I wrote about for the most part deal with that precious moment when we realise that life itself is precious, that there is something to savour in the ordinary. I wrote from those moments, out of a wounded heart, as a kind of therapy.

I only hope that what has proved cathartic for me will move the reader to laughter or tears or at least to ponder for a little while on the mysteries of life and love and birth and death.

In this collection there are memories of the benevolent simplicity of my own childhood in the west of Ireland alongside personal observations and recollections from my life as a teacher, a parent and, *mirabile dictu*, a grandparent. The collection contains some pieces that have previously been published in print and on radio.

My only sincere wish is that they will be enjoyed.

The Many-Splendoured Thing

It is a cold Saturday afternoon in late December and I have climbed into the attic. I'm supposed to be looking for last year's Christmas decorations, but that's only an excuse. I have really come up here to escape the pre-Christmas bedlam below.

This silent room above a bustling world is, for me, like the still point of a turning wheel. It is a space between past and present, under heaven and above the earth, free from conflict and tension, where I can sit and think.

I don't know about your attic, but mine is a repository of all that is useless and precious in my life. Things I should have thrown out long ago but couldn't, artefacts that have survived as we moved from house to house. In a place barely penetrated by light or sound, they lie like ghostly guardians of the past.

I move apprehensively between the tea chests and cardboard boxes that lurk here in the shadows. Surrounded by old familiar things, I am wary of their power. A tattered schoolbag, a school exercise book whose soft pages once opened on a world of wonder, a tin box containing a white seashell. A smooth stone taken from a windy western beach. Why do we keep things? Why are these the things we keep?

As I look around me the slanted sunbeam from the

attic window picks out a blur of white far back beneath the eaves, something half-hidden by an old plastic Christmas tree. I reach in to find a pair of angel's wings, made from two wire coat hangers wrapped in white muslin. And Francis Thompson's poem comes to mind:

> The angels keep their ancient places;
> Turn but a stone, and start a wing!
> 'Tis ye, 'tis your estrangèd faces,
> That miss the many-splendoured thing.

I am drawn back to a Christmas play and a little girl, at the tender age of six, about to make her acting debut as an angel. She has just one sentence to say: 'Do not be afraid, Mary.' She has practised it for weeks, flitting about the house and singing, 'Do not be afraid, Mary'.

And now her big moment is approaching. She is bowing down in adoration, her forehead on the boards. There is an uneasy delay and then a slight commotion, as the teacher comes to rescue her. A shepherd has been standing on her hair. Now she trots towards the Virgin Mary and her baby, looking a little flustered.

'Do not be a-scared, Mary,' she says, caught midway between St. Luke's Gospel and *The Little House on the Prairie*. She smiles and moves away out of the light.

When she herself left the stage of this world many Christmases ago, there were people who said, 'She's an angel up in Heaven now, you know, you can be sure of that.' I must confess that it didn't mean much to me at that time. But now as I sit here in the gloom and ponder that Christmas past, their words come back to me, and so do hers – 'Do not be a-scared' – and once again a happy memory shelters me from the cold wind of grief.

And then I hear a muffled voice calling me from downstairs where angels fear to tread. It is my son, who wants me to give him money so that he can buy me a Christmas present.

Who knows? Maybe he'll buy me something useless that will warm me with laughter in the winter's gloom of some far-off future Christmas. It might even make it to the attic and become enshrined with all the other many-splendoured things.

A Poem Lovely as a Tree

It was twenty years ago and I was standing in the school corridor like every good principal teacher should, with a school bell in my hand. The junior infants were coming in from lunch break in the yard. I went into the cloakroom, and there I spotted the tiny girl hanging back at the end of the line. She still had her coat on. Tousled hair, bright eyes shining out of the gloom.

' Come on, Rosie, hang up your coat and go into class with the others.' But she turned away from me, still holding her bright red coat tightly around her. She was holding something inside her coat, and it was not small.

'What have you got there, Rosie?'

She held tighter still. No answer, only a blank stare straight back at me. Then, finally, with the resignation of a child who realises that adults usually get their way in the end, she hung her head and opened her coat.

A piece of a tree fell out onto the tiled floor of the cloakroom.

I say a piece of a tree. Not a twig. Not a polished piece of wood, but a jagged broken branch of brown thorn tree.

'Rosie, Rosie! You can't bring things like that into the classroom. You might hurt yourself. What do you want it for?'

No answer, just the bright eyes looking back at me.

I picked up the old branch and determined to find the caretaker. Things like this should have been cleared from the yard. Children could trip over them. We could be sued for negligence. But before I could stride away to fulfill my vital role as administrator, Rosie gave me 'that look'. Parents will know what I mean. It was a look that said, ' You stole my stuff. I will never forgive you.' Then she turned and went into the classroom with the others, her head held high. Unlike me, she still had her dignity.

I was left alone in the cloakroom, holding an old piece of wood. Inside, I could hear the familiar sounds of education. The click of plastic disks and the singsong words in unison, 'Triangle, rectangle, square.' This is what we teach them; love of order and logic. Stuff to help them understand the world we live in.

But I wondered what Rosie was thinking. She had found something that she liked and had it taken from her. For reasons nobody else could understand she had looked on the ugly and thought it beautiful, worth keeping, somehow. What was it for? It didn't have to have a use to be valuable to her. It was something broken, something nobody else wanted.

I often remember that gloomy March day, and I often wonder where Rosie is today. I like to believe that she is a nurse, maybe, caring for the elderly or the unwanted. I hope she got through life without being trapped by the ordered and the logical.

And I hope she has forgiven me.

Penates

My wife likes to drag me along to view old houses that are on the market. We move in file from room to room with all the other invaders. When we emerge, my wife poses the usual questions as to what I thought of the size of the sitting room or the colour of the wallpaper. I am usually quite hopeless at remembering. But I always know whether I could be happy there. It's a matter of feeling. I know whether the household gods are friendly. The Romans had a name for them; '*Penates*', they called them, the spirits who guarded the home. You feel their presence when you cross the threshold.

When I'm not looking at the colour of the wallpaper I'm scanning the old photographs on the wall, photographs of milestones in a life. Communion, daughter's wedding, grandchildren. I like to escape to the garage. There is more reality here. What is it that they kept? Why did they keep it? Our lives are marked by what we keep and what we throw away. The dusty sunbeams pick out old toys, an old cricket bat, maybe, or a broken tennis racket. There is an old wooden stepladder and a neat row of rusting, cobwebbed tools hanging on the wall. Here is sadness and here is regret, and loss of innocence and the coming on of old age. I see contentment, maybe, a man who sprayed the roses and pinned them back, a man who could fix and mend until old age stiffened him and the wooden stepladder there became a mountain. The *penates* have a stronger presence here, where association and memory mingle.

In the house again, hurriedly painted for the viewing, I see a smudge on the architrave and I think of Séamas Ó Néill's fine poem about the jam stain his little son left on the newly-painted door. How he, the father, curbed his irritation and thought of the time when the doorpost would be clean and the little hand would be long gone.

> *Bhí subh mhilis*
> *Ar bhoschrann an dorais*
> *Ach mhúch mé an corraí*
> *Ionam a d'éirigh,*
> *Mar smaoinigh mé ar an lá*
> *A bheas an bhoschrann glan,*
> *Agus an lámh bheag*
> *Ar iarraidh.*

And then, inevitably, I start thinking of my own home and my own household gods. Our children, too, are gone. It is not hard to envisage a time when strangers will file in to disturb our household gods, strange faces peering into our past lives. And I think of the things I have lost and the things I have kept. What will they make of it all? What will they make of that rounded pebble from a beach, sitting there in a place of reverence on the mantelpiece? Will they connect it to a faded photograph of a small girl in the shadow of Croagh Patrick?

When you go into a house that has sheltered life, go softly. When you cross the threshold, pause, and sense the household gods. Wait for them to welcome you. If you are the right person, they will know, and so will you.

Festina Lente

The hotel corridor was quiet, carpeted. Polished mahogany doors on either side all shut tightly on other lives. Muffled sounds of human individuality and difference mixed with the staccato sound of television. It was evening time as I walked by the open door of her room just as she was emerging and heard her voice, so clear, so resolute, and with that intriguing, unmistakable hint of anger.

'It's always the same,' she said. 'You always manage to dilly dally at the end.'

I could only describe her as a stately old lady, her hair a steely silver, brushed back and permed, her eyes deep set and dark by contrast, her neck long and elegant. She fixed a soft pink scarf around her shoulders as she leaned forward in her wheelchair. There was a Burberry shawl folded and neatly spread across her lap.

Behind her, standing and picking up something off the dressing table, the man smiled faintly, catching my eye as I looked in. He was, perhaps, slightly younger, though stooped. He was well-dressed, with dark sleeked hair.

And then I passed along the corridor and only once looked back, to see him wheel her away towards the dining room. He picked a speck from her shawl as she continued to talk animatedly.

Sometimes we see things that are like a single piece of a jigsaw. A glimpse of the fullness of life condensed into an iota, an atom. Sometimes, unexpectedly, a story is no more, no longer, than a moment. And it leaves us so unsatisfied, so curious, that we cannot leave it there and accept it for what it is. A story is a shard from a broken vase, a stone sent spinning from the wheel of life. I wanted to follow them to the dining room and watch as he cared for her, settled her at the white cloth of the dining table, passed her plate and picked up her napkin when it fell. I wanted to hear a story maybe of love and sacrifice. I wanted to know about her anger and his soft look. But I knew also that I had no right to seek completeness and that a real story is more powerful when it remains untold. The mystery becomes the message. We look back on our own lives, do we not, as we would look at an old silent film, disjointed frames flickering against the bright screen of our triumphs and the grey background of regret. And we get no more than a glimpse of the lives of others, and we piece together the frames of their existence, and we fill in the rest.

Still I hold that picture of the woman in the wheelchair, the irony of her haste, the quiet compliance of her companion. For some unknown reason it has stayed with me and filled me with a kind of warmth.

'All I Really Need to Know I Learned in Kindergarten'

One of my favourite words of all time is the word 'kindergarten'. It conjures up such a wondrous picture of that first learning space we give our children: 'Kindergarten', German for 'the children's garden.'

And recently when I came across a book called *All I Really Need to Know I Learned in Kindergarten*, I just had to buy it. A man called Robert Fulghum wrote it and it's a book about life, about simple truth and everyday living.

These are the things I learned in kindergarten, Fulghum says:

Share everything.

Play fair.

Don't hit people.

Put things back where you found them.

Clean up your own mess.

Don't take things that aren't yours.

Say you're sorry when you hurt somebody.

Wash your hands before you eat.

Everything you need to know is in there somewhere, Fulghum reminds us, the golden rule and love and basic sanitation. Ecology and politics and equality and sane living.

And you can't argue with his thesis. Just think how

much better off the world would be if we lived by those rules. If we all shared everything and played fair. If we all, including governments, had a basic policy always to put things back where we found them and cleaned up our own mess.

I often wonder at what precise stage children stop doing as we say and start imitating what we do. And I think that it is only in the world of childhood that the secret of the world lies. To a child a promise is an empty thing; their joy is in the now.

There was once a time when people could live happily by the wisdom of the child. The Blasket Islanders were the rearguard of such a race, unsullied by sophistication. *An t-Oileánach*, Tomás Ó Criomhthain's account of the last inhabitants, contains a quotation that has remained with me always. He tells of the arduous journey to the mainland to sell the cattle, and how, after the fair, they contemplated going home to the hardship and the hard work of the island. No, said an older man in the company, they would wait another day and rest and enjoy a drink while they could. '*Lá d'ár saol é*,' he said, 'It's a day in our life.'

The Roman poet Horace said the same thing in another language. '*Carpe diem*,' he said, 'Seize the day.' Live in the now.

They say that all true artists create from that inner stillness of the present moment. Wordsworth was such a one:

My heart leaps up when I behold
A rainbow in the sky:
So was it when my life began;
So be it when I shall grow old,
Or let me die!
The child is father of the man.

And when the path of life is fading near the end, we know that there is often drawn around us a sheltering veil of simplicity, a 'second childhood' we sometimes call it. We leave the wilderness and come back into the children's garden.

All we ever need to know we learned in kindergarten.

You Can Talk to a Fire

Last Christmas I was visiting somebody in a nursing home. It was a bright, airy place, everything clean and shiny as a new pin. Aluminium windows keeping out the cold. Polished tiles on the floor. In a large sitting room old ladies sat around in a circle, rugs on laps, looking at but not listening to the television. There was a sense of calm and capable efficiency. A chirpy white-haired lady gave me a nodding smile as I passed her chair. The kind of smile that draws you closer. So I pulled up a chair and we talked.

'Yes, I'm very lucky to be here,' she said in answer to my opening question. 'They're very nice. They look after me really well.'

Then she was silent for a while. 'But I miss my own sitting room. And most of all I miss the open fire. I never let it out, you know. Not ever,' she said enthusiastically, her little eyes twinkling. 'I kindled it from the first few little coals in the morning. Then at night I would bank it up real high and just sit in front of it.'

She spread her hands in front of her, as if warming them before invisible flames. She was quiet now, but it was a quietness that conquered invisibility.

It was a silence that projected a picture without words and cast it clearly in my vision.

I saw a red-brick house that had long sheltered life, that had echoed the sound of a baby's laugh. A house that had seen joy and sorrow. She would have kept it spotless: lace curtains on the windows; a tiled fireplace with old faded photographs on the mantelpiece.

And of course, that big, banked coal fire glowing red and yellow with peaks and valleys of flame. I could almost see the light reflected in her eyes as she spoke.

She spoke of children, and grandchildren, as if memory of life and fire were one.

'My children are all gone now. It's a pity they never knew what I was like when I was young. I never got a chance to tell them.' She smiled wistfully. Then, quick as a flash, she looked me straight in the eye and said, 'You can talk to a fire, you know.'

Her words hit me like a chastening bolt from the blue. I myself was lost for words.

I just sat there and looked around me at the hanging baubles and blinking lights of the artificial Christmas tree in the corner.

I left her there with her frail fingers still spread out towards the wall, the wistful look lingering in her eye.

Sometimes we encounter wisdom in strange places, and we are stunned by the sudden revelation that life has another dimension above and beyond us.

Last Christmas, as a kind of tribute to that new-found wisdom, I did keep the fire blazing on the hearth. I kindled it and tended it and banked it up high. But I never managed to talk to it. Not everyone has the gift.

Stream of Memory

There is something about a river that captures the imagination, that appeals to the subconscious, as if our lives were one with the stream, having a spring and a flow and then a final ending where it is lost in a great expansive anonymity. And I believe that each of us has a special relationship in our mind with a particular river. Water moving through the earth in a relentless flow seems to echo our own journey from birth to death, from a tiny beginning to a place where we disappear into uncertainty, where there is something surely that remains of us, but in some vague, amorphous other form.

In my life there is such a river, or rather a stream, too small and insignificant to have a name, but I like to call it my stream of memory. It ran through our farm in the days of my childhood, born somewhere in the marly *fáslachs* of Carrowbeg bog, where the snipe and the curlew and the teal-duck held sway. There were pike there too, in the plashy pools and silvery streamlets, but we never saw them – just a quick splash of a tail and a darting through the sedge and silvery grass, a shaking of the reeds and they were gone. We knew of older boys who hunted them with pitchforks, but my father said that a big pike could swallow a baby, so we never stepped barefooted into those glassy troughs.

The water from this dark and desolate upland stretch of bog drained into a turlough beyond our mearing wall and then became our drain, our stream, and in our boyhood imaginations our singing river. It began tamely, snaking through the *Léana Mór*, where the cowslips grew and where the cows drank on balmy summer days, swishing their tails to keep the horseflies at bay and standing belly-deep in the water to ward off the dreaded warble-fly. When they broke the banks and clogged the flowing water, my father would cut the soft sides steep again with the hay-knife, and we would pull out all the chickweed and rushes with a long-handled fork, which he had specially turned at the forge to make a drag.

Where the placid stream left the flat land and flowed under the limestone wall by the sycamore, it ran faster, downhill through a rocky field called *Poll Na Bracha*. It narrowed and twisted and bubbled over the stones. There, at the little cish, we held our boat races. Our boats were tins with names like 'John West', 'Zam-Buk' and 'Sloan's Liniment', and they seldom made it far downstream without capsizing.

Where the stream slowed down again to a round curve under the beech trees, there was a shady spot barely mottled with sunshine where the yellow primroses grew between the mossy rocks. Sometimes our older sister came with us to this secluded spot to pick the fragrant flowers. She exists now only in that place, beside the quiet river, the flowers in her white hand.

Where that little river finally left our land through

the high, shadowed arch under the road from Headford, there was a cool, gleaming, wet-walled cavern, lit only by the dancing reflection of the low sun. There we would sneak, barefoot, and listen to the talk of grown-ups on the road above us. The soft, blurred voices of those vanished people drift down to me still, echoing in the cavern of my memory, the undulating pitch of their voices matched by the ebb and flow of the river, the dancing sun on the water.

My brothers soon grew old enough to help my father in the fields and I was left alone to roam the banks and hide under the road, but it was never the same, somehow. My older sister even sent me a blue and yellow plastic sailing boat to replace the old rusty racing tins, but the boat sailed too far and disappeared down the shore under the mearing wall, and though I ran frantically up and down along the whole length of the wall and even waited at the other end until nightfall, I never saw it again. I lay awake in bed at night while the wind moaned in the thatch wondering where shores led to. Did they go right down to the centre of the earth? Was there a blue and yellow plastic boat sailing alone in some pitch-black cavern where light never shone?

The thought haunted my childish dreams until I came across a poem in my school reader called 'The Brook', by Alfred Lord Tennyson. The poem exorcised my nightmare forever. All streams lead to rivers and all rivers lead to the sea, and the sea somehow pells freedom. And as long as the bright ship of your childhood can stay afloat in your dreams, you need have no fear:

> And out again I curve and flow,
> To join the brimming river,
> For men may come and men may go,
> But I go on for ever.

An Inspector Calls

Our school was a small, three-roomed, country school in north Galway. Not far from the shores of Lough Corrib. Not many people came to visit, not even inspectors. But whenever they did appear, they struck terror into the hearts of teachers and pupils alike.

In those days inspectors were officious, overbearing men who liked to impress everybody with their own importance. They were former teachers and they prided themselves in their own ability to teach; felt that that was the reason they were promoted. Teachers fawned on them. They could write a bad report in the school records that would remain a blot on a teacher's career forever. Pupils feared them. They knew that if they let the teacher down there would be hell to pay.

We were doing Geography when the inspector stuck his head in the door. It was a day of high wind and relentless rain, slanting in from the lake. Nobody had heard the inspector's car.

After he had hung up his steaming coat and hat by the fire and spent some time poring over the roll book he decided he would show off his teaching skills. Because of the day that was in it, I suppose, he took a Geography lesson about rain in the west of Ireland. It was all to do with the prevailing wind from the Atlantic, carrying the clouds. He made copious diagrams on the blackboard. Snapped his fingers at the teacher for coloured chalk. He drew a very good map of Ireland, not like the vague thing our teacher could manage, which looked like a fat dog begging for a bone. Lots of arrows coming in from the west. Then a cross-section with fluffy clouds trying to make it over the pointed mountains of Connemara.

He explained at length how the moisture-laden clouds have to climb into the cold atmosphere to pass over the mountains and so shed rain on the eastern side. This seemed to be the most important point of all; the eastern side got more rain. Lots of little dots falling on the right-hand side of the mountain on the blackboard. Very impressive.

Now for the tour de force. He would show off how well he had taught, while the teacher cringed in admirsation.

The inspector rattled off some quick-fire questions around the class.

'What direction is the prevailing wind?'

'Why do the clouds have to rise high into the atmosphere?'

'Why do they lose their moisture?'

So far so good.

'On which side of the Connemara mountains does most rain fall? He points to George. No answer.

'What's your name?'

Fear is palpable in the room now. Will pupil and teacher be written into the records, forever shamed for generations to come?

'Tell me now, George,' the inspector continues, waving his left arm with a flourish at the impressive diagram, 'which side of the mountains is the wettest?'

'The outside.' George replied.

After that answer, no other answer seemed to matter somehow. The Inspector seemed to lose air a bit like the deflated clouds on the eastern side of the Connemara mountains. Our teacher seemed strangely satisfied.

The driving rain stopped, the sun came out and we were released into the yard to play. When we came back in the inspector had gone and the teacher was in a buoyant mood. For some strange reason, George seemed to be his favourite pupil from that day on.

A Little Corner with a Little Book

*I have sought for happiness everywhere, but I
have found it nowhere except in a little corner
with a little book.*

Thomas à Kempis

There are many people, some well known to me, who
have never read a book. I can only imagine what a loss
that must be for them. I cannot comprehend what my
life would have been like without having been given the
gift of reading. I am thankful that my parents and older
brothers and sisters passed on to me a love of books and
reading and all things printed.

We were read to as children. After being washed
and fed at night we sat with shins to the fire while the
scrubbed skin turned a mottled red. The first book I
remember my sister reading aloud was *The Children of
the New Forest* by Captain Marryat. I still remember the
names of the four children whose father was killed by
the Roundheads: Edward, Humphrey, Alice and Edith,
and how they were saved from their burning house and
brought to live in the forest by an old forester called
Jacob Armitage. He taught the boys how to hunt deer
and the girls how to sow vegetables and cook and clean,

and he taught them, too, how to pull together and survive on frugality, and it all seemed to us then so appropriate and right. We longed to be like those boys hunting deer in the forest and hiding from the Roundheads and following imperceptible trails. I can see, through the mist of hundreds of forgotten books that I have since read, some of the illustrations from that old, well-thumbed book. Edward, a boy dressed in strange Cavalier clothes, holding his hands to heaven and crying, 'Has all England gone craven?' And I can see another picture of an arm poking through a small window to fire a pistol.

In the sleepy hollow of our feather beds we dreamed and lived the lives of those Cavalier children from another age and another history. On days under the sun and the wide sky we were children of the New Forest, shouting heavenward from the grassy knoll of the High Graffa, 'Has all England gone craven?' We had swords of peeled hazel and helmets of folded paper and when we hid motionless in the hay-filled loft of the barn the ones who milked the cows below us were the Roundheads, and they would hang, draw and quarter us if we made a sound.

Our older brother read us *Robin Hood* and *Treasure Island* and *Hereward the Wake*, and we learned of new dangers and lived new lives in the carthouse and the turf shed and atop the bench of straw in the haggard. Our fantasies were filled with new faces and we had our image of them in our heads only: Blind Pew tap-tapping to the door of the inn and Little John and Hereward the Saxon king. We fought with the longbow and the quarterstaff and the cutlass. Our doubloons were bottle tops which we hid in a tin box under a hawthorn tree by the stream. We drew a map on a torn-out page of a copybook.

Books came in parcels from our uncle in America. In the days of summer, I longed for the deluge of rain that would come sweeping in over the Maamturk Mountains so that we would get a respite from the beet field or the drudgery of hay, and I could read *Uncle Tom's Cabin* and *Kidnapped* and *The Swiss Family Robinson* and anything else that I was fortunate enough to find. I read books about life in English boarding schools, like *Tom Brown's Schooldays* and *Ashwood to the Rescue* and learned about tuck boxes and detention and pillow fights and a strange game called cricket. My brothers and I even tried to play the game ourselves, with made-up rules and home-made bats and three hazel sticks in the ground.

My father read at every opportunity, sitting in the big Windsor chair in the arch of the fireplace, under the oil lamp at night, or by the front window in the days of drumming rain. He had no great regard for politics, so newspapers only seemed to make him angry. He preferred books. He read the books of Maurice Walsh – *Blackcock's Feather*, *The Key Above the Door* and *The Road to Nowhere* – but his favourite author of all time was Zane Grey. He read all his books, over and over, and then we read them and learned new words like 'mesa' and 'gulch' that made us feel that we were much smarter than our friends when we played cowboys behind the rocks in the high meadow.

Reading these books in the quietness of our sheltered home seemed to fill us boys with indescribable, explosive energy. We ran into the fields and through the lanes and over the walls as if we had been charged with a potent drug. Our minds raced ahead of our bodies; the years ahead of us could not possibly arrive on time. We who waited in the fields had new lands to explore and worlds to conquer and we did not want to wait.

A Food for All Seasons

As I walked through the city the other day I couldn't help but notice that everywhere I looked there seemed to be a picture of a giant hamburger. I began to wonder if I was hungry, though I had barely finished breakfast.

And then I got to thinking of growing up long ago in the green valley in Galway and the way that our appetites were sharpened and shaped by the seasons. That old world around us gave us a food for all seasons. We ate with the clock of the year, our hunger sated by whatever the day provided.

Beyond the haggard near our house was a small orchard, with a little wooden gate that opened onto a paradise of sweet smells and pink and white blossoms and tastes that startled our untutored tongues with ecstasy. It was a place where shafts of green light tumbled into small clearings, where the wind was tamed into a whisper, where the thud of an apple on the grass would startle you into thinking that there were spirits here of a special kind.

In mid-summer, we gorged on the gooseberries and blackcurrants that grew in tangled plenty beneath the apple trees. Their tartness furred our tongues, but we made them into a feast. We pinched the eyes out of the fat blackcurrants and laid them on a saucer. We covered them with a ton of sugar and a spoonful of cream stolen from the warm pail in the dairy and settled down in the waving grass for our feast.

There were giant green cooking apples in that land of plenty, and bitter crabs for making jelly, but there was one tree of sweet apples that were our blissful bounty. 'Beauty of Bath' we were told they were, and they were beauties of a kind to us never to be repeated, a red and orange streaked hardness, a crunching, juicy sweetness on the innocent tongue of childhood. All summer we waited for their ripeness, sometimes perched in the branches, dappled by the green sun that filtered through the sinewy leaves, sometimes crouched underneath in the spidery grass, staring skyward to where they hung and swayed tantalisingly above us.

Then, as if by ordination, a hazy August morning would bring a whiff of ripeness, a solemn pronouncement from somewhere above that the bountiful harvest was here at last.

The fields, too, that surrounded us gave up their seasonal treasure, sometimes sudden and unexpected. A probing hayfork might pull up a bees' nest in the meadow. We would mark the spot with a handful of hay, return like thieves in the dewy evening and pull out the honeycomb to slurp the golden nectar that tasted of clover and sweet meadow grass.

In the first hazy mornings of July, when the sun spread its rosy light on the knee-high fog in the fields, we went forth in the startling coldness of the air to stir the cows for milking. As we tried to bully them from their munching peace and drive their swaggering forms to the yard, we rubbed our sleep-encrusted eyes and watched out for the first mushrooms. When they appeared, overnight, like manna from heaven, we each raced to our own corner of a field, where there were millions last year and nobody knew, only to find that the vein of plenty had changed this year, and there was a new bounteous slope somewhere else. We each staked our territory, kept it secret, carried our prize crop home speared on a plantain stalk, like a string of white pearls from a green sea.

There were brambles along the hedgerows, hung heavy in September with blackberries, dark and juicy and untainted, with soft flesh like sweet wine on the tongue. In the brown days of early October, the dying year yielded up to us a new taste. As soon as the word was out, we emptied the books out of our satchels and headed to Carnacrow Wood to pick hazel nuts. There, in the russet clearings, the ripe nuts would have shelled already and fallen on the mossy ground. We picked them first, then climbed into the branches for the nuts that still wore their half-tunic of green. If they shelled easily, they were ripe; if their coats were obstinate they were unripe. We pulled them anyway, regardless of their readiness. This was one of the days of plenty; we might never be here again. The spinning world might stop and we might never know the sweetness of the sin of gluttony. We sat on the rocks under the whispering hazel and broke the shells with stones. Some kernels were sweet as honey, some were raw as a cabbage stalk. It didn't matter to us, we relished old and new, sweet and sour. We filled our satchels and brought them home. We vowed to save some for Halloween, but we seldom succeeded.

I often think of those days when we were children on the unsullied earth, when the balance in our bellies was the balance of the seasons, when our diet was dictated by the turning world. And I sometimes wonder, too, what it would have been like if we had hamburgers.

A Corner of France

There is a sense in which holidays exist only in the past; in memory, in photographs, in traces of ourselves that no one can ever see or touch. Wherever we go, we leave part of ourselves, like some chrysalis shedding an unseen scale, and return, expended and exhausted, but somehow reborn. For seven years in succession, when our five children were small, we trooped to France for two weeks, packed so tightly into our old red station wagon that only heads appeared above piles of everything. On the very first day of the school holidays, we rushed to Dún Laoghaire for the boat. From the word 'go' it was all about staking territory, finding a space, and bristling if a stranger attempted to encroach. We closed ranks; we were the geese and the goslings venturing on the pond together for the first time. We swore silently at the deckhand who seemed to let all the other cars off the boat first. We crawled through the winding roads of North Wales and hurtled down the M1 at crazy speeds, miraculously dodging swaying trucks and weaving maniacs in high-powered cars. We fought over map-reading at Kew Bridge and Hangar Lane and Roehampton. At my sister's house in Wimbledon we tumbled stiffly out of the car and felt a thousand eyes watching us from behind lace curtains, marvelling that so many could fit in a car that was already full of luggage. We dragged cosy children out of their sleeping bags in the grey light of dawn the next day to head down the A3 to Newhaven and the boat to France.

After another stomach-churning boat ride we chugged our chock-full way through the labyrinth of Dieppe and kept right-hand side behind crawling caravans to Rouen, where we got lost again and blamed each other and all the time the silent question in the mind: 'Why are we doing this? Until finally, as the Normandy sun dipped low, we came to St Manvieu Le Bocage, a dot on the Michelin map, a village hidden deep among the apple orchards and high hedgerows of Calvados.

'Où est la ferme de Madame Leboucher?' was the sentence we had practised, but we couldn't fathom a word of the reply except to follow wild gesticulations to find, eventually, the house we had rented, a converted barn half-way between everywhere with beds that broke our backs and mosquitoes that dive-bombed us in the pitch-black, sweaty darkness of the night.

That first family holiday in France defined every other holiday like a headline in a copybook. The others were practised and planned, but they never could compare. It was like a child's first steps, faltering and fraught with inevitable disaster, but exhilarating and adventurous and new. For a family, it was a misplacement, a straining of bonds that served only to tighten and secure.

The children were lost in this strange new world in

the middle of nowhere, with nothing to do but play. For a while they were disgruntled and fractious: no television or familiar friends from school; no security of well-known street corners. Then they settled into a new way, finding birds' nests in the hedges and buying crispy baguettes in the ravenous, fresh-aired mornings and swimming in the coolness of the river. At night we played cards and told ghost stories by an open fire on the hearth, and flickering shadows of our own childhood mingled and danced with theirs.

During those two weeks' holidays we hacked out a new clearing in the jungle of our lives and we each took away something, or left something behind that would make a difference, no matter how overgrown that space became. Memories are the only indestructible things, however faint or fragile they become. Memories, too, for Monsieur and Madame Leboucher, of a pale-skinned family five times larger than their own who were crazy enough to travel from an island four hundred miles away and pay them a thousand francs a week to live in their barn.

And there are the photographs, freezing time in a moment, proving that it was not all a strange and shadowy dream. Photographs of two children playing with dolls on a stone step, children who spoke strange tongues to each other but who wept when they parted. Photographs of a smiling boy holding up a fish three inches long. A hazy picture of a pensive girl on a swing, caught in mid-air memory. These images do not occupy a separate place in our memory like some box of mementoes in the attic. They infiltrate our spirit like a coloured thread running through the tangled grey sleeve of our subconscious. They come back to us slyly, with a certain smell, or a fleeting look in the eye, or a cloud tinged with copper light, or the sound of children playing on a summer evening. Children grow up and families scatter, and people change, and die, but that first family holiday leaves too many traces ever to fade away.

Photographs

Time doth transfix the flourish set on youth,
And delves the parallels on Beauty's brow;
Feeds on the rarities of Nature's truth,
And nothing stands but for her scythe to
mow.

Shakespeare's sonnet brings me back through days and distance to the schoolroom with the high windows in the west of Ireland long ago, where we struggled with Latin verbs and the vagaries of the ablative absolute. Our Latin teacher never succeeded in teaching us very much Latin, but he was a teacher I was lucky to have and he taught us about life and waking into a world that was changing at a dizzy pace in those last dying days of the 1950s.

And he taught us about time.

Like most teachers of his era he was strict and diligent – we learned or suffered the consequences – but he was more interested in ideas than in facts and he was easily diverted from the narrow confines of the curriculum that sought to bind him. He loved to discuss films and plays he had seen and he revelled in the moral dilemmas that faced Fletcher Christian and Brutus and Hamlet, Prince of Denmark. He wanted to share his experience with us, and we tried our best to encourage him as often as possible. Anything was better than Latin grammar.

Which brings me to that memorable morning when he was at his best. We were struggling with Roman history, and the Punic War and Hannibal's army marching on Rome, and a wily Roman general called Fabius Cunctator, which means, as I recall, 'the one who delays'. Fabius just lurked in the hills and waited for another opportunity to attack, infuriating the poor Carthaginians and finally wearing them down and saving Rome in the process. I suppose he was one of the first exponents of guerrilla warfare. Time was on his side, you see.

And, of course, we got talking of time and what it meant to different people and then he asked the basic question 'What is time?' so we really had to think, and he loved to see us wrestle with the concept in our own simple way.

Think of a photograph of the class,' he said, 'and another you might take after a moment's passing. What would be the difference? Somebody would have moved.'

And led by that thoughtful man we came to the conclusion that time is really a measurement of movement or change. We calculate the movement of the earth and divide it into units with names like 'days' and 'years'. But if there was no movement, there would be no such thing as time. By way of illustration he produced a newspaper from his desk and showed us a great action picture from the sports page of a horse in full flight over Beecher's Brook.

'A photograph freezes all movement,' he said.

'A photograph conquers time.'

Those of us who have lost somebody precious know how right he was. When, suddenly, many years later, death snatched a child from us, one of our first mesmerised reactions was to scour the house for photographs, for evidence that she had once been among us. There were never enough of them; shots of camping trips and dressing up for Hallowe'en and opening presents on Christmas morning, each picture more precious than a jewel. Time frozen in a moment; moments locked in the memory. A photograph conquers time.

A Place for Everything

One of my mother's favourite sayings was, 'A place for everything and everything in its place.'

I am at that certain age now when I can't remember where I left things. I'm sure there are many readers out there who will sympathise. 'Where did I put my glasses? Where is that bill I should have paid last month? I told myself I was putting it in a safe place.'

We all have safe places for things, I suppose, places where we know we'll find them eventually. The trouble is that we are distracted and sometimes defeated by intervening life. Our safe places become precarious after all.

Watching sad events in New Orleans at the time of the hurricane I could not help but focus on the scattered things in houses; everyday things, papers, photographs, cutlery, children's toys. I kept thinking of the sudden departure, the choices that had to be quick and ruthless. What did they decide to bring, what to leave in each echoing well of loneliness? What will they miss most? How quickly and on what grounds did they decide between the replaceable and the precious? In some cases there were people who had to walk out and leave everything just as they had put them down.

A couple of years ago, my sister died. She had battled

illness bravely; rearing her children and seeing them leave, looking after her husband to the last. She was a real home-maker. Her house was always ordered and harmonious. Whatever she acquired seemed to be there solely to weave a cocoon of certainty around her house and its occupants. Now I sat in the living room of her house as she was being brought to hospital for what turned out to be the last time.

It was, indeed, a living room. Warm coals in the fire; a magazine, opened at a certain page; slippers on the floor, a lamp throwing soft light on to an easy chair, everything shaped to her comfort. Things were exactly where she had put them down and they would remain there, as if awaiting her return. I have kept in my mind the memory of that room as a memory of her, knowing that the moving of any object there would be a disturbance. These things as they were left will, in a sense, please nobody else. They will be bereft of usefulness somehow, like a long outmoded invention. They were there for her alone.

And I think again of the once happy people of New Orleans and all other places where death and disaster suddenly intervene in a flash, leaving so many things, so many traces of so many lives. Maybe I'm becoming morbid or fatalistic, but very often now when I leave down something precious I wonder if this is where it will remain.

And 'precious', for me, has taken on a whole new meaning.

Foreign Fields

When we got linked up to the Internet, my son, a child of the electronic age, helped me take my first faltering steps on to the information highway. I know that if I press the right keys a message will appear from my brother in Wichita, Kansas, four and a half thousand miles away. I had made up my mind that nothing would surprise me, but I was wrong. The surprise was my brother's e-mail address, staring back at me from the screen like a ghost. It read: 'hygraffa@westwinds.net'. To any Internet user, that term 'hygraffa' wouldn't mean a thing, but it certainly did to me. My brother had chosen this electronic code word carefully.

High Graffa was the name of a field beside the house where we were born, a field that was all a hill, with a row of hawthorn trees sheltering us from the wild west wind. Our childhood was plotted and pieced in fields, each one with a name and a shape and a history: *Gort na Ceartan* meant 'the field of the Forge'. We found old rusted horseshoes there in the red clay as we thinned the turnips.

There was a Low Graffa too, sloping down to the marshy land of *Poll na Brafa*, where a small stream drained away the floods and a little stone bridge provided a magical place for us to hide our treasure when the dry months of summer came. We hid a quarter-pound of Yorkshire Toffees there once, sealed in a biscuit tin, and planned a hoard for the future. But after ten minutes my brother decided that we should save up only hard sweets. We ate the lot and left the tin to rust away forever.

My father knew the measurement of every field, in acres, roods and perches.

'How did they measure them?' I asked him one day as he ploughed the *Leath-Cheathrú*. It was such a crooked field that it took all his skill to negotiate the headland.

'Trigonometry,' he answered, with a look of deep wisdom in his eyes and a reverence for those who went before him.

My father loved his fields as if they were a living part of his own body. He remembered their yield and plotted their crop rotation. Under his watchful eye we picked the clover-stones that might damage the mowing machine and pulled up the yellow *bráiste* weed from the green oats in June. He rebuilt the limestone walls when they breached and added to them with the brown rocks that the plough dug up. Here and there he could point out to us the trace of a built-up door, or an ivy-covered archway that once housed a fireplace. He would say:

> A time there was, 'ere Ireland's griefs began,
> Whenever every rood of ground maintained
>   its man,

The only time I ever saw him cry, we were digging potatoes out of the cold wet November soil of *Gort a' Lochta* beside the road. My brother was leaving home, cycling away, with his suitcase, like his future, balanced precariously in front of him. Maybe my father knew, even then, that this was the end of an era, that, no matter how much he taught us, we would all leave, one by one.

I should be watching the Internet screen now, but I only see *Páirc Bheag*, the tiny field with the high walls where I used to hide from everything but the sky, and lie on my back among the yellow cowslips and taste the purple clover and look up at the singing lark disappearing in the clouds.

I don't think they have any clouds over Wichita, Kansas – or any fields either, only prairies, stretching away to the end of time. My father wouldn't like that.

I don't blame my own son for getting impatient with me, as I sit staring at the screen, but there is a poem by Monk Gibbon going round and round in my head:

> Who would have thought a little field,
> A far-off road, a far-off lane,
> A far-off cottage could in time
> Wake far-off thoughts with so much pain,
> Wake far-off thoughts so hard to stem
> A man might fear to think of them?

A Strong and Perfect Christian

When we were schoolchildren long ago the sacrament of Confirmation held out the prospect of great humiliation. Up at the altar rails, in front of the whole neighbourhood and the bishop himself, you faced your own defining moment. You answered a Catechism question at the top of your voice while the world around you stood still and held its breath. If you got it right, the Catechism said you became 'a strong and perfect Christian'.

I was in fifth class, decked out in a wine-coloured blazer my sister had bought in Clery's. And I wore my first long trousers. Presents of beads and prayer books and scapulars and medals had rained down on me from aunts and uncles I had hardly even heard of. We had practised Catechism, Bible history, Catechism notes and every possible twist and turn of our religious knowledge at school for weeks on end, until I felt that I knew a much as the priest himself.

The church was packed to the rafters, full of the pomp and ceremony of the braided bishop in his mitre and staff. Triumphant hymns shook the walls; incense hung like ether in the perspiring air. Pale, starched schoolchildren trembled like jelly. Someone fainted and fell, a head full of Catechism cracking the floor like a coconut. Some children were examined by the priests, who flitted about like flies. A rumour went round the seats like a breeze that the bishop would examine only Sixth Class. I was devastated. How could I show off my knowledge now? It was all very disappointing.

A lithe, bony-faced priest with sleek, oiled hair swooped on our pew. 'I think we are supposed to go up to the bishop, Father,' I said timidly, not wanting him to make a mistake.

'Oh, really?' he replied sarcastically. 'Am I not good enough for you?'

The way he said 'good' made me feel as small as a threepenny bit. I lowered my head in respectful humility.

He let the silence hang like a judgement in the air.

'What is presumption?' he snapped, fixing me with a cold stare.

I stared back at him like a rabbit caught in the headlights, frozen with cold fear. He was bent over me, his face so close that I could tell he had had a boiled egg for breakfast. 'Well?' he persisted.

I was flattened. My mind was blank as a slate, all the tangled weave of learned answers gone like a cobweb in a stream. It was different when the master asked the questions in school. I could rattle off the answers like clockwork. Perspiration oozed from my forehead and my new shirt collar tightened like a noose.

The priest straightened up to look at the sixth class trooping up to the bishop. 'Just as well you're not going up there to make a fool of yourself,' he said archly.

Then someone behind me whispered the word 'false'.

And I was off like a hare, blurting out the answer like a kettle boiling over: 'Presumption is a false expectation of salvation without making proper use of the necessary means to obtain it.'

'And don't you forget it, sonny,' the priest said, pointing his finger like a gun at the centre of my forehead.

When he was gone, I turned around to find out who had rescued me from the dead. It was a girl called Veronica. She sat there with her golden ringlets and her white veil like a vision of the Virgin Mary. She lowered her beautiful blue eyes and smiled shyly, and from that blessed moment on I was confirmed a weak and imperfect Christian. On my way down from the altar, having had my cheek stroked by the bishop, I saw only her among the blurred, hazy throng that packed the church. I swaggered home in my long trousers and wine-coloured blazer intoxicated with the smell of the new-mown hay, my mind racing ahead like thistledown on the warm summer breeze. Sitting in the old master's classroom, across from the girls, across from Veronica, would never, ever be the same again.

A Taste of Where We've Been

My wife and I were touring South Africa. We had passed over the spectacular Tradouw Pass in the Western Cape, heading east through the Little Karoo towards Oudtshoorn and on to the Garden Route. When we came to the sleepy town of Barrydale, set in a little green valley between the bare hills, we decided to halt for a while. The temperature outside was thirty-nine degrees and the African sun was reaching its zenith. We turned off the main road down on to a dirt track and followed the sign that said, 'Take a break at the Blue Cow. You will not be disappointed.'

The 'Blue Cow' turned out to be a handsome wooden structure beside a small man-make lake shored up by a dam. We were welcomed by the proprietor, a tall, vivacious lady who almost overwhelmed us with talk and with kindness. As we sat at our table on the terrace overlooking the surrounding fruit farms we talked about the heat and how it was so different from the soft rain in Ireland where we came from.

'My great grandmother came from Ireland,' she said, her eyes lighting up as she placed a stunning platter of assorted meats, goat's cheese and salad in front of us. 'She came all the way out here just after the potato famine; married a Dutch farmer near the Cape. They came up here in their ox wagon, over the Langeberg, even before the Tradouw Pass was made. Our farm is just over there.' A cool breeze from the fields fanned our cheeks, lifting the corners of the white linen tablecloth.

The rest of our meal was served by a beautiful black girl who told us her name was Melody. She moved with gentle grace around the table and her smile lit up the soft shadows of the room. When our host came back, she spoke about the uncertainty of the future. 'The weather can be merciless here. Two years ago there was a terrible hail storm. It wiped all the fruit from our trees. And the future here in Africa is so uncertain.' Her voice seemed to trail off and she looked away into the distance, over the purple mountains.

Melody cheerfully cleared our table and accepted the tip offered with genuine delight. From the shelves of the restaurant we bought a little pot of orange marmalade: local produce, a taste of where we had been.

Two weeks later, we are about to head for the airport in Cape Town and our luggage is formidable. We will have to make a sacrifice for the sake of the great silver bird. I bundle up, among other things, my unopened pot of marmalade from the Blue Cow and push it into a bin by the road. As I move off in the traffic I notice, in my rear view mirror, a thin, dishevelled black man rummage there. He takes out the pot of marmalade, puts it in his bag, looks around him and walks quickly away.

As the plane banks over the beautiful flat top of Table Mountain and heads north we breathe a sigh of relief that our baggage has not been too heavy. Still, we are sorry that we have left behind a taste of where we've been.

Captured by Freedom

Eamonn loved walking along O'Connell Street in his ordinary clothes. He liked the hustle and bustle, the way people rushed about not even knowing he was there. It was mid-July 1960, the sun was shining and he was free for the summer. All thoughts of the dark cloisters of Maynooth Seminary were banished by the gay brightness of the city and the constant roar of double-decker buses, the shouts of news vendors and the babble of pedestrians who shuffled and pushed their way through the teeming pavements.

He had just climbed to the top of Nelson's Pillar and looked out over the sprawling city. He had watched the gulls wheeling and diving, their white wings carving the dark rain clouds and he had envied them. He had looked down the dizzying distance to the streets underneath until the old dark thoughts came back again and he had moved warily back from the edge. When he eventually came down the winding stone steps he felt he was descending into a dungeon and almost panicked, until he emerged into the brightness of the day.

He had stood outside McDowells, the 'Happy Ring House' for a long time, looking in at the sparkling jewellery and the young couple at the counter inside. They looked into each other's eyes. She laughed, throwing back her head and shaking out her long blond hair. The young man looked so confident, taking her hand in his, fitting on the ring. He could not hear their words or their laughter. He felt so outside of everything. He saw his pale reflection in the glass of the window and he backed away into the path of a hurrying pedestrian and had to mumble an apology.

It was his mother who sent him to Maynooth. She had had it in her mind for as long as he could remember. 'Oh, Eamonn's my pride and joy! Eamonn is going to join the priesthood.' That was how he had always been introduced to strangers since he had made his First Communion. As a child it had meant only that he knew what life had in store when he grew up. Then everything had become so ingrained, so settled, as if a will had been made and it was unalterable and bound by some sacred precept. His mother shed tears of joy. 'I'm so proud of you in your soutane. My own flesh and blood, a priest of God! Your father is up in heaven smiling down at you!'

His father, a quiet, inoffensive man, had died of TB just before Eamonn's Leaving Cert. The only thing that could console his mother was that, 'Eamonn will look out for him in the afterlife. Only for that I don't know what I'd do!'

Many times, especially in the quiet of the night, he tried to analyse his own self. Was it that he was too complacent, too kind-hearted? Was it just a matter of not wanting to offend anybody? Was the priesthood what he really wanted? It was something that he did not really understand, but then he really did not understand himself. He always found it easier to go along with what his mother said. She probably knew what was best for him.

And so the time came round, the clothes were bought, the doors of the seminary opened wide and another obedient servant passed inside.

It was just outside Clery's that it happened. One minute she was walking in front of him and the next minute he was almost on top of her, his arms around her waist and the smell of her perfume enveloping him. He would always remember the feel of that camel-hair coat, the depth of her dark eyes as she looked back and down at him, the flash of red lipstick.

'It's my high heel,' she said. 'It's stuck in the damn grill.'

It all happened in a moment, outside his existence, as if he were still standing outside the jeweller's. But his imagination had now become the actor, the '*deus ex machina*'. His hands were cradling the rounded leather heel, twisting it. 'Mind my leg, you're twisting it.' In that one moment he took in the authority of the voice. Not like his mother's authority, more of an assurance, a confidence. All in that magic moment he looked upwards and she pulled a tweed skirt aside to look down at him and he saw...

He would reflect many times and in many ways on what it was that he saw that day as he knelt on the iron bars of a grill on the pavement in O'Connell Street while the world hurried by. He saw the sweet gates of sin, he saw the light of freedom framed by the blue sky above, he saw the pagan world of human love and he was captured forever.

When she asked him to join her for a cup of coffee in Clery's restaurant he had no power to refuse. When she told him about her life in that sophisticated city he had no choice but to listen in rapt attention. When she picked up the white cubes of sugar her red nails mesmerised him. Her name was Paula and she was, 'young to be a lonely widow at twenty-nine'. 'It was TB,' she said, but her voice was void of grief. He looked downward at the silver coffee-pot, he gathered the crumbs on the white linen tablecloth, almost afraid to look into her dark eyes, in fear that all this would suddenly come to an end. She questioned him very little and he told her as little as ever he could. And when she asked him if he would like to go to the Gate Theatre with her some evening that week he stepped out of an old world and willingly walked down the sweet slope into the blissful garden of human desire.

And every year of their happy married life I know they celebrate this day of July with a cup of coffee in Clery's. And though they had no children and they missed that, they had time for each other, time to analyse their good fortune and talk and joke about the day when they had rescued and captured each other.

All for Diaries

'Nobody should keep a diary or an autograph book either,' my mother said. 'The written word remains.'

I had just cycled the three miles home from secondary school, by the honeysuckle's smell in the hedges, to a dinner of fried potatoes and thick, home-cured rashers. Whatever about the odd parental lecture, at least I didn't have to face incarceration in a freezing boarding school. Three years earlier, the nuns had taken a courageous leap forward by admitting boys into the local convent day school. God only knows what heated exchanges had taken place in mother houses and wainscoted diocesan rooms. This was the west of Ireland, it was the mid-1950s, and we were the first co-educational secondary school west of the Shannon.

The pioneering nuns took us in, country louts that we were, dusted the hayseed away and gave us Latin and French and apologetics and pi-times-the-radius-squared. In no time at all we could match the girls in every subject. If only we could have communicated with them.

The girl who owned the diary was from the town. She sat in front of me in class and when she laughed, she threw back her head and the ends of her blonde hair just touched the top of my desk. She could never do a geometry cut, but she went to grown-up dances in the town hall, and she could jive better than anyone I knew. Her diary, which had a red padded cover with a gold clasp, also had a special pull-out section for autographs, and this was the one that was passed around the class.

Now maybe we were too shy to converse with the girls face to face, but given that vital few moments' reflection, we could communicate our thoughts in writing. Terrible, wild thoughts, things we could never dream of saying. Words borrowed from the street corner on a fair day, where we had learned terms and tales we scarcely understood. We signed our names under daring lines of lewdness. Then, of course, came the inevitable seizure by the vigilant nun and the fearful court martial afterwards.

I remember waiting with sweaty palms for my turn to face the inquisition. Death seemed like a welcome alternative to the possibility of disclosure. Luckily, my contribution was quite low on the Richter scale of shockingness. The letter home was mild enough.

Looking back now, there was really very little to cause a raised eyebrow, but the guardians of innocence were vigilant in those days and the least crack in the sea wall was sealed quickly to ward off any threat that might exist from an unknown tide.

Many years have slipped by since then, and I'm rummaging through that old shoebox at the top of my wardrobe – the thing I would look for if I knew the house was on fire. There is a diary here that I'm glad I have. Words written by a child of mine who must have found it easier to write them than to say them. Though she's no longer here, her words, defeating time and space, will stay with me forever.

That's why I'm all for diaries.

Let the written word remain.

Charlie Penny

It was the summer of 1968 when I first went to New York. I was a nineteen-year-old student, working on a J1 Visa for the summer. It was a turbulent time in America, a time of assassinations and riots, and, of course, the Vietnam War. But life went on in that great teeming city, and I was in search of a job.

In a pub in the Bronx I met a man from Connemara. Before telling me about his plans to return one day to the land of his youth, he gave me the name of a friend who might be able to give me a job.

'Take the Coney Island subway downtown and look for the White Rock Soda Corporation on Washington Street. Ask for Joe. The thing is you gotta shape up for work each mornin'.' I pretended to know what he meant by 'shaping up',

Next morning in the dilapidated docklands of the Lower East Side I found my first job on foreign soil. And I soon found out what 'shapin' up for work' was. You gave your name to the guy in charge, he looked you up and down and you stood there in a group. If your name was called there was work for you. If not you went home. I was assigned as helper on the truck driven by a lanky, thirty-five-year-old black man called Charlie Penny.

Charlie Penny and I got on like a house on fire. He

made fun of my pale skin and because I was a greenhorn, hardly knowing the difference between a nickel and a dime, lost in that great melting-pot of a city that he thought of as the centre of the universe. He was young and streetwise and he swayed rather than walked, as if moving in time to an unheard melody.

His driving was as undulating as his walk. Together we careered crazily through the streets of Lower Manhattan, our high truck laden with cases of soft drinks, some of which I had never heard of, like root beer and Dr Pepper's. In all the terror of traffic Charlie Penny never lost his cool. When the drivers of the yellow taxis shook their fists at him he just laughed and when he laughed his whole body shook like a leaf.

The next morning in the yard of the White Rock Corporation I did not have to 'shape up' for work. Charlie just picked me out from the crowd and yelled, 'You're the man!' All that hot month of June we shunted cases of soft drinks all over downtown New York, to lunch bars in Wall Street and little shops in side streets off Times Square, the pale-skinned greenhorn from Galway, Ireland, and the cool dude from Harlem. He wanted me to tell him all about growing up on a farm in Ireland. Until he was fifteen years old, he said, he had never seen the stars at night.

One Monday morning, Charlie did not show up, and I was out of a work. I eventually got a job in construction and our ways parted, but when September came and it was almost time to head back home to Ireland, I took the Coney Island subway down to the waterfront to see my newfound friend. When I asked the boss he said, 'Charlie Penny? He got drafted. He's gone to fight the Viet Cong.'

The following day, as my plane banked over the skyscrapers of New York and headed east towards the green shores of Shannon I thought of cultures and how they meet and mingle and coalesce and clash and I wondered if a fun-loving cool dude like Charlie Penny could ever bring himself to kill a man.

Four Ducks on a Pond

I saw a death in the paper the other day, of a man who went to school with me. He left home when he was fifteen, worked on the buildings in England for most of his life, moved from London to Wolverhampton to Coventry, wherever there was work. He was a labourer, a hard, honest worker. He lived hard too, never married, slept rough, drank a lot, and never came home to the west of Ireland, to the shores of Lough Corrib where he and I grew up.

I can still picture his smiling face in the classroom. I remember that he loved the open spaces more than the books. Most of all he loved the lake, which lapped softly by the fields of the small farm where he was reared. Every year he missed school for three weeks in May, in the dapping season. He gathered mayflies on the shore, sold them for a penny each to anglers in tweed hats. He brought me with him once, and I watched him pick the green-winged creatures delicately out of the hawthorn where they hid from everything except his eagle eye.

And, of course, I met him again, once more in our lives, that day in London. I was a student, working for a summer on the buildings in London. On Saturday night I joined the mayhem that was the Irish pub in Camden Town and there he recognised me, picked me out of the milling crowd as skillfully as he would pick a mayfly out of a hawthorn. And we drank together and he drank a lot, and the more he drank the more his childhood enveloped him like a sweet mist. He put his arm around me, and, looking at me with glazed eyes he mumbled the words:

> Four ducks on a pond,
> A grass-bank beyond…

It was a poem we had learned together in school. He told me it was the only poem in the world he could ever remember. And he told me how, on a bitterly cold winter's day, as he worked in a freezing, mucky hole on some waterlogged building site, a brace of wild duck had alighted on a grey pool beside where he worked. And suddenly the words of the poem came to him out of nowhere:

> Four ducks on a pond…

And he wept, then and there, remembering the softer water of the Corrib and the gentler breezes that blew in from Inchequinn, carrying the mayfly on to the thorn.

And William Allingham may have cried too, touched with sadness, when he composed those simple lines as a young immigrant from his native Ballyshannon. His circumstances were more congenial but his loneliness was the same.

Poetry, like music, crosses barriers of time and class and distance, and it has the power to move us, no matter who or where we are. And a simple poem of seven lines can shake us as much as an epic. So for my childhood friend I speak the lines reverently, simple lines in memory of a simple man:

> Four ducks on a pond
> A grass-bank beyond
> A blue sky of spring
> White clouds on the wing:
> What a little thing
> To remember for years
> To remember with tears!

Here Is the News

I have a friend who has given up listening to the news. He doesn't read the papers any more either. I think I understand why he feels that way.

Listening to the news can make us angry and helpless: so much injustice in the world, so much needless suffering, and so much that we cannot change. So many seemingly good men and women who are exposed as criminals, sex fiends, embezzlers. So many politicians corrupt. Hunger and famine in the undeveloped world, war and terrorism everywhere, global warming, poisoned rivers, religious fanatics, rising inflation, inadequate hospitals.

And here we are, in our own world, with our own concerns, our own troubles within easy reach. Our thoughts are of our family and friends. My worries are my health, my days and nights growing shorter, my span of life running down. I have no room for anger and frustration about things I personally can neither reach nor change.

And I think of the old people I knew as I grew up in the west of Ireland. The news from the outside world, such as it was, was a mere ripple in the quietness that surrounded them.

My father told a story of long ago, in his father's time,

of a herdsman in the village. He was a simple man, a man of his time, quiet and inoffensive and willing. He looked after a small farm that my grandfather had leased on the other side of the town. He counted the cattle and sheep, tended to them when they needed care, reported regularly that everything was well.

'Have you any news, Johnny?' my grandfather would call out whenever he would see his herdsman approach. Invariably, there was nothing to report, and my grandfather would be pleased. On his next visit, again, the same question; 'Have you any news, Johnny?' my grandfather would ask, anxious about his stock, and the inevitable answer would come: 'Devil a bit.'

And then Johnny began to feel a little inadequate. He felt that he was disappointing his employer somehow. He should have something to report, something, however small or trifling, that would justify his trade, that would make him feel valued for his vigilance. And so the next day, for the first time in his life, he bought the newspaper and read the banner headlines emblazoned across the front page.

'Any news, Johnny? My grandfather called out as usual when he saw Johnny wheel his bicycle into the farmyard.

'I have, and bad news!' Johnny replied, with gravity in his voice and a solemn look on his brow.

'What is it?' my grandfather asked anxiously, thinking that his cattle had been stolen or that there was an outbreak of foot-and-mouth.

'The king of Portugal is dead,' Johnny replied.

From that day on my grandfather would always greet his herdsman with the phrase 'No news is good news, Johnny!' and Johnny never had to spend money on the newspaper any more. The outside world remained far away and irrelevant to the slow, easy pace of that remote rural landscape.

But sometimes when I hear of a shooting in Beirut or a riot in Kabul I think of that distant time and I think of the nature of knowledge and the way people were and whether missing out on the news would make any difference to our happiness at all.

From Another Bed

My sister died a few years ago. First ambulance doors, then endless stairs and disinfected corridors, had shut her off from the everyday business of her own life. Very soon there was only the supine staring at nothing but the suspended ceiling above the bed, and eventually the unreachable window, opening now on nothing but the sky.

But futile questions still linked her to her life, like limp fishing lines thrown out into a lake now draining steadily. 'Did someone pay the electricity bill? I never missed paying it on time. Never, ever. That Christmas tree will have to be thrown out. It was already beginning to shed, and I don't want the carpet ruined. What about the heating oil? There's very little left.' Those who visited her faced the daily questions, the daily concerns and all gave the daily reassurances.

And then there was one late afternoon when a low wintry sun seemed to turn everything rusty. Inside, the tubular light in the ward shone brighter than before as if to prove that it was more powerful, more permanent, than anything the natural world outside had to offer. She was lying back on her pillow, and her face had a look I had never seen before.

'Are you OK?

'I'm fine, fine.'

'You look different.'

'I feel different.'

Then silence for a while. Not exactly silence, though. A nurse was straightening the sheets on the bed in the corner diagonally across from us and under the window. She was very exact in what she did, turning down the tops of the sheets and tucking everything in place. She patted down the counterpane, put her hands on her hips, then picked up an invisible mote between thumb and forefinger and strode away with a satisfied look on her face. There was a strong smell of disinfectant, stronger than usual.

'I always wanted to be in that bed under the window,' my sister said. 'But it doesn't matter now.'

'What do you mean it doesn't matter? I'll ask…'

'No, no, you won't.' She held up her white hand. Then she took my hand in hers. Her skin had a wafer quality only. 'Do you remember her?' she asked, nodding towards the empty bed, 'the woman who was there yesterday? She died last night. I heard her dying. I didn't see her, but I heard her dying. And then I must have fallen asleep, because when I woke up I was in that bed, but I was looking over at myself in this bed. And I could see under it, and there was nothing.' She stared at me, searchingly, looking for a reaction. I could only return her look. Then she turned her face slowly towards the window and spoke softly but with a certainty that had been missing since she first heard of the inevitable.

'You know when I first came in here, before I knew…'
she paused and I tried to interrupt, but she held up her
hand again. 'I kept a mental note of all the things, all
the daily things, that I should be doing, like ordering
heating oil and paying the electricity bill and collecting
my pension. I imagined that I was putting all those
chores in a safe place so that I could tend to them when
I was going home…I imagined that I was storing them
all under the bed, that they were piled there, in a kind of
a bundle. And they kept me propped up, you might say.
And then, last night, from the dead woman's bed, I saw
that there was nothing there.'

'Nothing really matters,' she said, finally. 'It took me a
long time to realise it. Nothing really matters.'

The rest of my visit that evening was spent more or
less in silence. Not exactly an awkward silence, but a
silence resigned to awkwardness. I held her hand and
we both looked out the window, past the empty bed, and
saw the winter sun slowly dying against the glass.

When I finally stood up to go, she said, 'Could you do
me one favour before you go? Ask if there's a hairdresser.
I want to get my hair done.'

When she saw my incredulous look she half-smiled. 'I
know…I know,' she said. 'But I still want my hair done.'

Light My Fire

Her name was Helga, she was Swedish and she was beautiful. His name was Seán, he was a young teacher and like the rest of us he was new to the city and the ways of women. But he had a car. A Volkswagen Beatle, with split-back rear windows and only seventy thousand miles on the clock. He was the envy of us all.

The Four Provinces Ballroom was where we did our dancing. Every Sunday night we sweated and swayed there in that teeming mass of humanity. We jived so energetically that our heads spun and our shirts dripped off our backs. We danced so slowly and so close sometimes that everything in the world stood still except that one thing that drove us to distraction.

Yes, we were young teachers, 'the cream of the country' we were told, but it was nineteen sixty seven and our little world was being shaken and stirred by a revolution that we scarcely understood but which involved freedom and flowers in your hair. 'Light my fire, light my fire; come on baby, light my fire,' the Doors urged us from the great American stage, and we all burned in unison.

Seán met her there in the 'Four Ps' on a Saturday night and when we saw her from the balcony we were all filled with envy. She had long blond hair, a body like Cher and tanned skin that spoke of lying under the sun in an exposed manner. Seán certainly had a penchant for the exotic. He seemed to be able to shift the unshiftable. We reckoned he must have told her about the newly acquired Volkswagen Beetle with the split-back windows.

The following Saturday night we were to meet, as usual, in the Shakespeare pub in Parnell Square. It was not exactly the Ritz, but the pint was good and the plastic seats were comfortable. After much persuasion, Seán agreed to bring along Helga, the Princess of the North. It would add to our feelings of awakening into the world of cool international sophistication. In honour of the occasion, some of us ordered gin and tonic instead of the ubiquitous pint of porter. But the path to sophistication, like the path of true love, can be fraught with unexpected setbacks.

Seán duly picked up his prize exhibit at her lodgings in Raglan Road and sped off towards the north inner city to where his friends waited in drooling anticipation. All went well until he turned down into St Stephen's Green. The old engine missed a beat, coughed a couple of times, and then glided to a silent halt beside the kerb. Now Seán was no mechanic, but it did not take him long to figure out that he might be out of petrol. The trouble was, there was no way of telling for sure, because the old Beetle, the pride of German engineering, did not have a petrol gauge. They were probably a later addition. Perhaps in the de-luxe model.

To access the petrol cap, Seán had to open the

bonnet. Helga examined her newly painted nails in a kind of bemused detachment as Seán fumbled under the dashboard for the lever. When he lifted the bonnet and unscrewed the petrol-cap it was so dark that he could not peer into the tank to see if there was any petrol left there.

It was when he caught a glimpse of Helga through the windscreen that he made his rash, impetuous, fateful decision. She was gazing vacantly out the side window and Seán got the awful impression that she would rather be somewhere else. And so it was, as with many a hero before him from the time of ancient Greece, that reason deserted him, driven away forever by the pale shade of beauty. He lit a match to look into the tank.

There was a loud 'whoosh' as of the Holy Ghost descending on the Apostles and a flash of fire lasting a split second as the vapour inside exploded and Seán's face felt suddenly hot as a coal.

When they finally reached the pub there was a sharp intake of breath from the assembled crew, followed by a pregnant silence. But it was not the Nordic beauty who took the breath away. It was Seán's face, bright crimson as far as his ears only; eyebrows and eyelashes completely gone.

Finally, someone said, 'Jesus, Seán, you look like the tail light of a bike.'

For reasons untold, the romance between Seán and Helga did not last. Maybe she returned to her native Sweden. Maybe she wrote a book called *Romance in a Foreign City*. Personally, I think her love was tested too early in the relationship. She never stayed around long enough to see Seán's eyebrows grow back. As Shakespeare once said:

> Love is not love which alters when it
>   alteration finds,
> Or bends with the remover to remove…

All I know is that Seán's next girlfriend was from Kerry and that he traded in his old Beetle shortly afterwards for a Ford Anglia, complete with petrol gauge.

Heartstrings

My mother sat pensively by the fire, her head half-nodding in sleep, her frame bent and frail. I had gone home to visit her from Dublin with my wife and two youngest children. It was the year Caroline left us, so I know that it was two years before my mother died. Having reared ten children and seen many grandchildren come into the world she had virtually emptied herself of love and care for them. Now her energy and focus were slowly slipping away.

She was a remarkable woman. She spent her life in the quiet dedication to family that was so common then, never seeking her own comfort above those of her husband or children. Rearing a large family on a small farm in the 1930s and 1940s was a formidable challenge. Yet she never lost her good humour, her dignity, her dreaming.

For some reason my gaze focused now on her bony wrist as it shone waxen in the flickering firelight. While she fingered her rosary beads the sinews that radiated from wrist to knuckle worked rhythmically, undulating and shuttling beneath the skin with a shaky but resolute movement.

It was as if there before me was imprinted on her hand the outward image of her role as mother and minder of us all. From her wrist the sinews fanned outwards, as from the centre of her being she spun continuously all her life a web of lifelines spread out to each one of us, holding us to her, woven with the soft, warm fibre of her certainty, forged with the steel core of her love.

Her heartstrings never choked us, never tied us down, but we felt them when we walked the sinister street at night or wheeled precariously over the ocean at thirty thousand feet. When we, her children, brought our own children into the world and struggled uneasily to learn, we felt those heartstrings strum and vibrate with a conviction that all would be well, that somehow the web would save us. We were never alone.

And I thought there by the fireside that such is the nature of maternal love, such is the durability and indestructibility of the bond that exists in the umbilical cord. It is cut at birth but never severed: its body becomes its soul, refracted, invisible, and everlasting.

And I thought of my own dead child and that cord, too, now and forever indestructible.

The School Tour

The school bus was cruising along through the salu-
brious suburbs of south Dublin. The air was filled with
the noisy chatter of seven-and eight-year-olds on their
way to the farm. This was a new landscape for them,
very different from the stark, cheerless environment of
their own place. In the parlance of the Department of
Education, they were from a 'disadvantaged area'. It was
labelled so for definable reasons of social deprivation.
But I always struggled with the term itself. The younger
children in that stark, urban landscape where I had the
privilege to teach were the most genuine, real, authentic
children you could find, unvarnished by pretence or
affectation.

I sat at the top of the bus, having counted the heads
several times, making sure that we had a full cargo.
The young assistant teacher sat at the back, keeping
a watchful eye as always to see that everyone sat safely
in their place as the bus lurched and chugged towards
the freedom of field and sky. I relished days like these.
Being principal teacher meant that, too often, I was a
prisoner of the school office, away from the cutting edge
of interaction with the children. I missed the organised
chaos of the classroom where adult and child met face
to face, where troubles and joys were swapped and sub-

stituted, where all things real and imaginary blended in a magical, potent mix of listening and seeing and making and learning. Never again in their lives would there be such innocence or such candour and never so much again would they value and enjoy the care and love that was lavished on them by parents who often had only love to give.

As the bus drew to a halt at the traffic lights outside an enormous, three-storey red-brick house, I listened to the conversation between Gemma and Louise who sat directly behind me. Gemma was a beautiful, fair-haired child with bright blue eyes and a slight lisp. Her companion had long dark pigtails, each tied with a pink ribbon. Her face was freckled and there was a pair of wire spectacles perched on her nose.

'Look at the size of that house!'

'It's like a palace!

'If I lived there I'd have a room all to myself!'

'You'd have loads of room to play.'

'I'd love to live in a house like that!'

It was Gemma's turn to speak. There was a long pause. 'I wouldn't like to live there. Imagine my ma having to clean all them windows!'

Gemma's mother was a lovely, quiet industrious woman; young to be a mother of two. Her husband had left her to rear them by herself. She always had them turned out well, crisp and clean in their school uniforms. They were always first to buy their schoolbooks, never looked for assistance. Their home was a credit to her.

The bus took off from the traffic lights, leaving the big house behind. The two friends lapsed into silence and left me to ponder in silence too. Later that day after we had seen all the animals, there was the inevitable shopping to be done. When I watched Gemma count out her pennies to buy a porcelain jug that said, 'To the Best Mum in the World', I thought of how lucky some mothers are.

Who said educational tours are a waste of time?

'A Good Walk Spoiled'

It was an unclouded morning on the golf course. In the forest behind us, the bluebells and daffodils glistened with dew. There was a mistle thrush high up in the ash tree rinsing the crisp air with music. The grey city beneath us shimmered in the distance. Down there people were actually working, queuing in cars, rushing through offices and sweating on building sites.

We seemed to be above all that, in this golf course hewn out of the Dublin hills, where the deer come down to crop the fresh grass and drink in the rivulets that tumble from the high shoulder of Three Rock Mountain. In the untouched ravines, foxes and badgers run their rituals, and the coarse cry of the cock-pheasant echoes in the thicket. And, of course, there is the strangest species of all: man.

My playing partner has just played a bad shot. He thumps his club into the ground and curses roundly.

'My head was up again, God dammit!'

'I should have bloody well stayed in bed!'

But he knows, like the rest of the species, that he will be back for more punishment next week, hacking his way out of the undergrowth, complaining about the contrary wind, while all around him the buds pop on the yellow whins and the new primroses bask in sunny nooks under the red briar-leaf.

In the clubhouse, he and his friends will complain about the tracks of the deer on the greens and the wild meadow-grass that hid his lost ball.

Golfers are all the same.

Well, except for Harry. Harry is seventy-five years old, and he used to be an undertaker. Maybe that's what changed his view on life. The first time I met him, I asked him what was his handicap.

'I'm short, bald, I'm deaf and I have a s-s-s-stammer,' he said with a grin, 'But you'll get used to it.'

I had the most enjoyable round of golf I ever had that day with Harry.

His jokes were never-ending and we laughed to the sound of the birds' song. His cries of frustration were only in tune with the futile game we played. You could tell that he saw his own image for what it was, a passing shadow on the clear water of the mountain stream we crossed.

'Laughter is the only cure for grief,' he said when we had finished, as he gripped my hand firmly and looked deep into my eyes like a seer from a wiser world.

'When I die,' he said, 'I am going to have my ashes scattered here on the eighteenth fairway.'

I know him well enough to believe him.

I can visualise a dull breezy day on the hills. Solemn men in black suits upturning a silver urn. The wind from Three Rock Mountain will whip the ashes off the cultured grass into the wild trees, like it used to do with

Harry's golf ball, and his spirit will settle easily there, unchanged through the changing seasons, whispering to all the passing golfers.

'Head up ! Head up ! Look around you!'

It's the only way to play the game.

'If Music Be the Food of Love'

I had the good fortune recently to spend an evening with a wonderful couple called Tony and Jessica. He is a professional musician, she a professional masseuse. They have three equally wonderful children, and I'm sure that there will be no jealousy when I say that the youngest one, Jack, is special.

Jack is nine years old. When he was two and a half, he suddenly contracted meningitis. He lay in a coma for nine weeks, speechless, unmoving, and struggling for life. There was a shunt inserted into his brain to drain away the fluid that kept building up there. His young parents never left his side, and they never forgot their own natural talents that, for some fateful reason, were destined to bring their son back to them. They knew that if he lived, he would somehow seem, in the eyes of strangers, to be changed. They also knew that, to them, in the quiet shared chamber of their hearts, he would forever remain the same.

Jessica sat by his bedside, stroking his face and his arms, letting the familiarity of her maternal touch reach beyond the tubes and wires and dials of artificial life to caress the mysterious inner sleeping self. And his father sang him songs and strummed his guitar softly to him. When he could not physically be there he played him recorded music, the music that had, as a child made him dance, made his toddling body sway and rock back and forth in rhythm, made him smile and clap his hands. But now there was never the least stir, no movement, and no eyelid flutter, not one hopeful twitch of a finger or toe.

And then, one day, it happened.

Freddie Mercury, that's what happened. Freddie singing the chorus of 'We will, we will rock you' suddenly blared out loud and raucous at the sleeping child as it had done when he used to do his toddler dance. And suddenly now, out of that alien space balanced somewhere between life and death, Jack burst into a smile and his body shook and moved and life returned, riding on the back of song. To the joy of everyone he soon left hospital and music it was that made him better. Not just ordinary music, but the music that only lives by being shared, the kind that mixes memory and heartbreak and weaves them into some potent thing called love.

Like I said, I spent a great evening recently with Tony and Jessica and their family and a bunch of friends. And we had a right good singsong. And Tony, as ever, belted out the music, this time the music of James Taylor:

> You just call out my name,
> And you know wherever I am
> I'll come running,
> You've got a friend.

And I noticed that as Tony tapped his foot in time to the music of that song he tapped it on his son's foot, and at the same time his mother stroked the young boy's arm, and Jack smiled and clapped and revelled in the sweet sounds that were woven round him, drawing him in, making him safe, always reminding him of that blessed day when the warmth of music melted away the frozen world that tried to claim him.

In the words of Shakespeare, 'If music be the food of love, play on.'

The Boy who Bought the Complete Works of Shakespeare

When I was a student teacher forty years ago, St Patrick's College, Drumcondra was much different from what it is today. It still had its cloistered quadrangle and its high, noisy dormitories. It was an all-male institution, a melting pot of eighteen-year-old raw country lads, mainly from the western half of the country. They tended to band together in raucous groups depending on the boarding schools from which they had graduated: great diocesan colleges like St Brendan's, Killarney and St. Jarlath's College, Tuam; preparatory colleges such as Baile Mhúirne in Cork and Coláiste Éanna, Galway.

There were a few of us who had not gone to boarding school. I struck up a friendship with a fair-haired freckled youth from near Dromahair, County Leitrim, called John Joe Reynolds. We both drifted on the periphery of the *profanum vulgus* so we inevitably became friends.

When territory was being staked out in the clattering refectory we stuck resolutely together at the same table of eight, but when the dish of spuds was being passed around we found, on the first day or two, that it was empty by the time it came to us. Blows were almost struck. A country lad cannot survive without potatoes.

John Joe and I came up with a plan. One spud per man in each passing of the dish, then the dish was passed back in the opposite direction. The dish starts with a different man each day. Plan accepted after much debate, a victory for democracy, for power sharing, for the smaller parties.

Shared adversity brings people closer together. Occasionally we got a ten-shilling note in the weekly letter from home. When we were hungry we shared what we could.

Then, one day, out of the blue, John Joe got a letter from home with a twenty-pound note inside! An old aunt had died, God be good to her, and thought of him alone in the heartless city. I thought of things like a slap-up dinner maybe, in that hotel in Parnell Street where, they said, you could actually eat all you wanted. But I remember John Joe holding the big banknote tenderly against the light and smiling wistfully.

The following Saturday he came home from the city carrying a box. Sitting on his bed in the afternoon sunlight he opened the box and showed me what he had bought. Three red leather-bound volumes: *The Complete Works of Shakespeare*, fresh from Gill's Bookshop in O'Connell Street. 'Nineteen pounds, nine and six,' he said proudly. 'I still have ten and sixpence left.' When he saw the dismay in my face he said, 'If you buy food you eat it and it's gone. I'll always have these.'

When he left the training college he got a job in some remote two-teacher country school in Donegal and our ways inevitably parted, but I often imagined him walking up and down the echoing boards of a schoolroom while the class chant their tables and his brown, leather-clad volumes of Shakespeare sit proudly on the window ledge, a testament to his dreaming, to his belief in the great permanence of art.

Common Sense

I was buying a new coat in the winter sales in the heart of the city. The assistant, a young man in his early twenties, looked at me quizzically as he put the coat into a bag.

'You're Mr Walsh aren't you?' he asked. 'You taught me in sixth class.'

'Aren't you great now to remember me,' I said, feeling quite pleased that he had not forgotten his old schoolmaster.

'Oh, I would always remember you,' he said, as he closed the till on my money. There was something about his tone of voice that left me a little uneasy. I stepped out into the cold wintry weather pondering his words and stood for a moment on the pavement, a pensive old man buffeted by passing shoulders like some forlorn island in a turbulent stream. When I closed my eyes his child's face came back to me, from among a sea of upturned faces in a small crowded prefabricated classroom. In this crowded gallery of the memory the names are vague but underneath each individual face there is a label, a plate engraved and polished by me alone. The thin boy by the high window was 'good at maths'; that was 'a poor speller', the boy in the front row beside my desk; and the genial giant at the back whose father was an undertaker had told me that his father said he 'had enough education for his occupation'.

I find that I have classified them all by what they could or could not achieve, or else I remember them for one defining moment in their young lives, something they said or wrote that stayed with me through all the passing years. And I suppose the great adhesive of all memories is humour. It was Eoin Ryan who wrote in his Geography test that the equator was 'an imaginary lion running around the middle of the earth'. And wasn't it Declan Hannigan who pronounced to the class that Elizabeth I was a very thin woman but she was a very stout Protestant!

And standing at the bus stop in O'Connell Street, laughing away to myself, oblivious of the rain and the curious glances of the impatient shoppers, I thought of his name, the boy who sold me the coat. It was Joseph Kelly, and I remembered him because I remembered the day I tried to inspire him and the rest of the class to write meaningfully, to make their words come alive on the page. 'Remember you have five senses, boys. Whoever reads your composition should be able to see and hear and touch and smell and feel everything you are describing.' When it came to correction time Joseph Kelly read his opening line and it became his defining moment and singled him out forever in my memory. He read aloud, 'As I came down the creaking stairs in the bright morning I could smell my mother frying on the pan!'

As I journeyed home on the bus I wondered how

Joseph Kelly remembered me. Was it for some small act of recognition, some word or line, perhaps, that singled him out from the others like a sunbeam would in that dark, green gallery of a classroom. Or was it for the relentless efforts on my part to mould him into someone who could read and write so that he could buy and sell as well as any other?

I walked home from the bus stop in the evening drizzle, pondering the nature of learning and remembering the words of an old man cutting sedge on the side of the road to Ballyconeely who asked me what degrees I had from university. When I told him, he leaned on his scythe, sucked his pipe and said, 'Do you know what I am going to tell you now? None of them pieces of paper is any good if you have no common sense.'

When my wife opened the door for me she berated me loudly for going into town without a coat. 'Look at you,' she said, 'you're drenched!' I did not have the heart to tell her that I had a coat in my bag. I just muttered something about how we are never too old to learn.

Inclined to Rhyme

They are not long, the weeping and the
    laughter,
Love and desire and hate:
I think they have no portion in us
After we pass the gate.

Ernest Dowson's old poem comes to mind as I drive by the gate of the ivy-covered thatched farmhouse where I grew up. In this fine weather there should be people making hay, but now:

> The silence of unlaboured fields
> Lies like a judgement in the air.

Poetry always reminds me of my mother. I can see her now, bringing tea and soda bread out to that high meadow on a hot June day. My father is castigating a labourer who has failed to show up to help us with the hay. The labourer was a drunkard and a waster, we all agreed. All except my mother, that is. She quotes quietly:

> Who steals my purse steals trash,
> But he that filches from me my good name
> Robs me of that which not enriches him

And makes me poor indeed.

Well that shut us up all right. Not for the first time, my mother could make the words of the poets fit the world. She never went beyond primary school yet she could quote from Shakespeare's plays and Milton's *Paradise Lost*.

She was not unique in this respect. When our parents and grandparents learned poetry, they committed it to memory, and such learning enriched their lives as well as ours.

Gray's 'Elegy' and Goldsmith's 'Deserted Village' were the people's favourites.

> Full many a flower is born to blush unseen
> And waste its sweetness on the desert air...

she would say wistfully, or maybe:

> For of all sad words of tongue or pen
> The saddest are these: 'it might have been!'

It was pure wisdom packed tightly into verse, lines from the old lesson books that everybody seemed to know. But it was not all pragmatic. I remember a July evening, coming from the well, when we watched the sun set behind the islands of Lough Corrib and Gerald Griffin's poem sprang to her lips:

> On the ocean that hollows the rocks where
> ye dwell
> A shadowy land has appeared as they tell,
> Men thought it a region of sunshine and
> rest,
> And they called it Hy Brasil, the Isle of the
> Blest.

Poetry belonged to the people then, not to a chosen few. It lay lightly on the spirit.

Small wonder, in those green summers, that we, as children, were inclined to rhyme too.

The aforementioned labourer who was given to drink wandered into our house late one night and fell asleep on the hearth. During the night he felt the cold and put two sods of turf, as he thought, on the fire. In the morning my father found his new shoes burnt to a cinder.

As Homer's ghost whispered to Patrick Kavanagh: 'I made the Iliad from such a local row.'

The next day, as we crept along the drills thinning turnips, we composed our own epic in hushed voices.

> The night Pat Forde was on the booze,
> He burned my father's Sunday shoes.

Some years ago when my mother died I found among her papers a little book that I had never seen. It had a worn cover stitched on with white thread. It was Blackie's English Classics edition of 'The Deserted Village'. On the fly-leaf, her name, in fine curved copperplate; Anne Lee, Fifth Standard, July 12th, 1918.

As I looked out at the overgrown fields where we made hay, I didn't have to read the lines she would have quoted:

> Ill fares the land to hastening ills a prey
> Where wealth accumulates and men decay.

Marley's Ghost

The other day I picked up a marvellous edition of Dickens's *A Christmas Carol*, illustrated by P.J. Lynch. Those amazing drawings of Victorian London brought the book vividly to life again in my memory and brought me back to my first encounter with that magical story.

It was the last year of the 1950s. I was thirteen years old, it was my first year in secondary school and television had not yet come stalking into my imagination. Sister Rosario taught first-year English, struggling with what she saw, God be good to her memory, as our rustic lack of culture. She decided that a dose of Dickens was as good a way as any to introduce us to the great classics of English literature.

'Marley was dead, to begin with. There is no doubt whatever about that.' I can still see her cynical eyes ranging around the classroom, her pleading voice and her head shaking in despair, as each of us in turn read Dickens's opening lines. As we struggled with the words her blood pressure rose steadily and her round, shiny cheeks reddened and bulged against the confines of her starched white head-gear. But persistence and tenacity is the attribute of the nuns. As those impressionable days turned we got to live the counting house, the freezing streets of Victorian London, but above all, in the ripeness that was our pre-television imagination, we saw the ghosts.

Ghosts were easy to see then. We lived with them. They surrounded us in the pitch-black silence of our rooms at night. They walked with us on the twisty road home from the card game. We saw shapes in the stone walls, under the lone bush. We heard the wail of the banshee in the mournful whistle of the wind and we believed in the plight of the souls in Purgatory.

Small wonder, then, that Dickens's spirits burned on our consciousness so readily. The words of the master storyteller awakened in us all that which we dreaded most: Marley's face in the door knocker, the clanking of chains as his spirit came nearer and nearer from the cellar and, most horrible of all, 'when the phantom taking off the bandage round its head…its lower jaw dropped down upon its breast!' You see we had heard tell of the '*marbh fáisc*', the bandage wound round a dead man's head to keep his death-slackened jaw from opening.

Those words, that image, fastened itself to my memory. It flickered on my mind's eye every time darkness descended on me. If I woke in the fear-filled night I was sure, for a long, long time, to see that awful face from another world painted so vividly by the master wordsmith. Closing my eyes was no protection: the gruesome face burned all the brighter on the back of my eyelids. And even in the daylight landscape of those days of innocence and wonder there were places where the spirit world was revered and acknowledged. Quiet places, sometimes marked by a mound of earth or a lone mountain ash, places undisturbed by plough or harrow, where shadows were more than they seemed and the sigh of the wind in the dry stone walls was an ancient and eerie whisper. We did not play there in the summer days, where the air was laden with old stories of a world beyond ours that we did not understand.

Nowadays our children seem far removed from that other world. There are no spirits; there is no realm beyond the known. The old gods are gone. As for restless souls coming back, like Marley to make reparation? Bah! Humbug! We are the sceptical Scrooge, questioning the existence of the spirit, believing that there was 'more of gravy than of grave' about the apparition before his eyes. Our minds are much more in the counting-house.

But I suppose, like Dickens, I believe in the happy ending and I would like to think that, unlike the old skinflint, we have not yet become 'hard and sharp as flint, secret and self-contained, and solitary as an oyster...'

Where Mountainy Men Hath Sown

I suppose I've always been fascinated by fields. I don't mean the vast tracts of land between neatly trimmed hedges that you see from the car window in the plains of Royal Meath, but the tiny, irregular spaces bound by built limestone that lattice the high landscape of the western hills. If you go west from Cong to Maam Bridge over *Máimín na nGabhar* you will see them, or if you are driving west past Recess and look north towards *Doire Mhaoile Mháma*. High up in those precarious places there is something that rivets the eye, drawing it to a green space between stony ground where, as Pearse once put it:

> Mountainy men hath sown
> And soon would reap, near to the gate of
> Heaven.

I think of the building of these walls, high up on the mountain, the carrying of stone and the digging up of rock and the talk between men and women in those now lonely places. I often imagine the work there, the swish of scythe and the clink of spade against stone that would carry on the breeze and echo down into the valley. Here was no place for plough or harrow, only muscle and sweat and strain. I try to imagine a silent place where even the quiet word carried far, where there was no rupturing sound of motor or machine. How must it have been there in the summertime, up in that vast freshness where the wind filled your open mouth when you spoke and the lowland spread out under you like a part of your past life.

Today, if you look closely, you can still make out the abandoned potato ridges, now moss-covered, that lie like the mounds on an abandoned graveyard. There are ghosts that trek the shoulder of these high places. Men in high soft hats, women in swirling plaid shawls. Whenever the shadow of a cloud scuds across the mountain slope I think I see stooped forms. Spade on shoulder, bundle underarm, they move silently across that lost landscape, but they disappear again whenever the yellow sunlight glints off the granite outcrops of these lost places.

They are lost too in our history, lost in our memory. There came a time when the hills became hungry, when a bitterness came on the edge of the wind. The ghosts swapped the shade of clouds for the shadow of tall buildings in Boston and New York, where their faces became pale and strained.

'Where are the sun-dark faces now?' the Belfast poet Joseph Campbell asked.

> Grassland and lowing herds are good,
> But better human flesh and blood.

Recently I drove out the road that winds west from the crossroads at Liscarney and went by Leitir Brock and Drummin. I climbed the great sleeping shoulder of Sheaffry Mountain and there, by the crumbling gable-end of a ruined cottage I found, half-hidden by briars, the rusting blade of a *láidhe* (loy). The wind from the mountain seemed to whisper the words of the poet:

> The silence of unlaboured fields
> Lies like a judgement in the air:
> A human voice is never heard:
> The sighing grass is everywhere.

Off By Heart

My neighbour's little boy is nine years old and his mother is worried about his back. No, he doesn't have a congenital ailment. It's just that he has twenty-seven books in his schoolbag. Oh, and a set of mathematical instruments. And a calculator. Knowing him, he probably sneaks his Game Boy in there as well when his mum is not looking.

This will come as no consolation to his mother, but when I was that boy's age I had four books in my satchel. Irish, English, Catechism and a copy of the *New Progress Arithmetic*. History was in the teacher's head. We listened in rapt attention as he told dramatic stories like the escape of Red Hugh O'Donnell from Dublin Castle. Geography lived in the big smoke-stained map of Ireland that hung on the easel at the top of the classroom. We made the perilous journey there to point out the Knockmealdown Mountains or trace the course of the Munster Blackwater.

I suppose it's just that the nature of knowledge has changed. Certainly the nature of learning has.

And the scope of the imagination.

I can close my eyes and still see the simple line drawings by Eileen Coughlan that graced our school books then. I can see 'The Old Woman of the Roads' in her shawl, on a stone-walled winding road leading to a thatched cottage by the hill.

I see a black ink drawing of '*Sean-Mhaitias ina shuí le h-ais a dhorais*' while the village children played in a ring before him, the haloed 'Iosagán' in their midst.

These images are still etched clearly in my mind's eye; still potent in spite of passing years.

And, of course, there were bright passages of prose, and there was poetry and there was learning 'off by heart'.

'Off by heart' was the great philosophy, the mantra of our learning days. I have often thought about that expression. Not 'off by mind' or 'off by brain', but 'off by heart'. The feeling heart was the right receptacle, the place where music and poetry feel most at home, the place to store what we scarcely understood then, but which we would treasure in later life.

And it is the reason why my heart, like the collective heart of my generation, is full of old poems. And it is that collective heart and not the written page that has kept them alive.

Whenever my heart is hungry for beauty, or inspiration, or whenever I feel alone, those lines surface again out of the mist of time and surround me like old friends would in time of trouble.

> I remember, I remember
> The house where I was born,
> The little window where the sun

Came peeping in at morn…

'OOPS! There I go again.

Well, I suppose there are worse afflictions than having your head full of old poems you learned in school. At least it's no great load to carry. Come to think of it, it's a lot lighter than carrying twenty-seven books on your back.

Mind Your Language

On the 46A bus into Dublin city the other day I sat behind a young woman and her baby. She spoke softly to her infant, sheltering him beneath her shawl. The words were foreign to my ears, comforting to his, making him look up and smile into her dark eyes. I tried to make out the language, it sounded Russian, or Slavonic, I could only guess.

I thought how wonderful a language is, how lucky that child was, to have words woven around him that made him unique in a world of strangers, yet known to his own. He will easily recognise his mother's call from outside the schoolyard. If she is lonely he will have the right words to comfort her. If he grows up here he will never remember his mother's birthplace, but he will have the speech of his forebears, the words they used when they were young like him. Their own language will always be their badge and their bond.

And I remembered the days of my own childhood, and the remnants of the Irish language that my parents still spoke in the *breac-ghaeltacht* where I grew up. My mother's quiet voice by the bedside; '*Téigh a codladh, a chuisle. Ná bí ag caoineadh.*' My father naming the wild flowers: '*lus an chrom chinn*', '*cam an ime*', '*bainne bó bleacht*'. A language clings like love, dies doggedly, surfaces in times of deep feeling.

And I have a fond memory of an August evening in the early sixties in the highlands of Scotland. It was the year of the Cuban crisis and the Russians, we thought, were our enemies. I was a teenager, backpacking with my good friend Michael Breen from Listowel, staying overnight in a youth hostel in Kyle of Loughalsh. The dormitory was a melting pot of nationalities, a Tower of Babel of tongues. The lights had been turned out but young people talked loudly to their own in English, German, Dutch, and Scandinavian. We were trying to get some sleep.

'*Téigh a codladh! Tá mé tuirseach,*' I called loudly from the top bunk.

'*Agus mise freisin,*' Michael replied from below. '*Tá sé déanach!*'

There was a slight hush from the other occupants. A different sound. A foreign tongue?

'*Cad a dhéanfaimid feasta gan adhmad?*' I asked.

'*Tá deireadh na gcoillte ar lár,*' he replied.

Each time we spoke we gathered a little more silence around us. By the time we had got to the end of the first verse of '*Cill Cais*' there were just a few quiet murmurs to be heard, and then, gradually, sleep stole quietly down in the breathing darkness.

I turned and looked out over the dreaming moonlit highlands of Scotland. Ironically, there were crofters out there who would have understood what we said. We have an old bond. An Indo-European thing, even. Our

Celtic language was heard in the foothills of Yugoslavia long before many other European languages evolved.

The following morning, over the pots and pans, I struck up a conversation with a young Londoner.

'I think there was a couple of Russians 'ere last night. Amazin', ain't it? Hope they wasn't spies!'

I just smiled, for the first time in my life really proud to be different.

Patience

He had to use the stick now to get up from the armchair beside the fire. He reached up to the beam across the ceiling for the pack of cards. The big beam was the mainstay of the house, you might say. It was as if it supported all that the house had stood for all the years and held the roof together. It was a permanent reminder of the time when his great-grandfather hauled it up from the bog and set it there between the two side walls. The shotgun used to hang there, when it was safe to have a gun in the house.

He settled himself at the end of the kitchen table. It was where he always sat: the head of the household, the master and mover of all that happened. Maggie at his left-hand side, eldest son at his right, others in order of appearance, you might say. Their ghosts surrounded him now, though they were more like shadows, really. Their faces and form, which had changed so much with the years, were blurred by the confusion of passing time.

The dusk was easing into night outside the kitchen window to his left. A grey crow pecked at something in the field by the road. He hated crows as vermin, remembering the time when they would pluck out the eyes of a newborn lamb and he would go after them with the gun in a furious rage, clambering over walls as high as a house. Now there were no lambs, and there was no rage left in him. The grey crow could do no more damage.

It was an old pack, brown with the smoke of the kitchen, some cards bent at the edges. He shuffled the cards between his calloused fingers. They had lasted a long time, through rousing, raucous, lively games of twenty-five, when neighbours used to call and they would play five single hands or partners maybe and there would be rows and arguments about reneging or not following the trump and voices would be raised and fists crashed on the table. But it was the great sound of human intercourse, and he missed it with a deep ache, and it was gone now, drowned by the ticking of the clock.

He dealt the cards in front of him on the shiny oilcloth; seven cards in a row, first card turned up. A black jack on a red queen, nothing else to move yet. He had always called it 'Patience', though his son-in-law, who was from London, called it some name like 'Solitary'. He himself was never a man renowned for his patience. Six of clubs on the seven of hearts; seven children, all gone out into the wide world, their mother in the nursing home; maybe 'Solitary' was a better name.

Whenever the run of the cards defeated him he looked out the window, trying to get a glimpse of the road through the gathering gloom. A car passed slowly, its headlights sweeping left and right as it followed the twists of the road, then dipped and disappeared downwards into darkness over Clover Hill on its way towards the village. Jimmy Lyons used to call for him sometimes and bring him in for a few pints to Morans, but it became awkward after a while, what with the two sticks getting in and out of the car, not to mention the unbendable knee. It never recovered from the day he lifted that stone on to the gate pier of the *Léana Mór*.

He did not like to drink alone, at home. It only made him feel more alone than ever. His sons used to bring him out when they came home with their young children. That was a good time, too, the chatter and laughter of grandchildren breathing new life into the old house, but it, too, passed quickly.

The one thing, the one solitary thing, you might say, that left him wounded, was the thought of the farm, the land, the space and footprint of the people that went before him. What had been bequeathed to him as a sacred entity was now unused, neglected, It lay inside him and weighed him down like some heavy, decaying inner carcass. It all seemed so futile now, all the building of walls, all that tilling and clearing and weeding.

He shuffled the worn cards again, ready to replay the game. All around him, the old kitchen absorbed his gaze. The game of 'Patience': a game for the solitary: another tilt at the futile. What need had he to be patient now? What was it that he was waiting for?

It was almost completely dark outside the window now, and he could see his hunched frame reflected in the glass, the emptiness of the kitchen behind him. 'The lambs are weaned,' he muttered to himself. 'The birds have flown the nest. Maybe 'Solitary' is all that is due the propagator in the end.

But loneliness is another thing altogether.

Black queen on a red king…

Pulling up Roots

It's that time of year again when dandelions show their yellow heads above the grass and daisies are appearing on the lawn. I am told it's time to operate.

For someone who was born and reared on a small farm in that bountiful era before we ever heard of pesticides, this ought to be minor surgery, but it has a disturbing effect on me. I pull up my past with the roots. The smell of the wet clay brings me back to a beet field bounded by limestone walls. There are drills of sugar beet stretching ahead of me. Weeks ago the little plants pushed through the top of the brown drills; now they stretch ahead of us, all bright green and glossy with recent rain. And they are choking with weeds. There are five of us – my three older brothers, my father and I – on our knees, crawling in the earth, thinning the fledgling plants and weeding around them. The hot June sun is above us and the smell of growth is all around. We have to leave one small seedling at spaces of about nine inches, pull up the surplus plants and make sure that all the weeds are pulled as well.

My father's voice carries back to me on the soft breeze as I lag behind the others: 'Make sure you pull the roots. We don't want to see them growing again behind us.'

I am the reluctant son of the soil. I do not want to be there. It's all right for the others, but I am only nine years old. I have a rag-nail that I am trying to bite, spitting out the salty earth that clings to my fingers. My knees are bound in hemp bags, tied above and below the knee with binder twine, but I can still feel the hardness of the stones as I crawl painfully along. My father, up ahead, leans over to my drill and thins a bit for me so that I am now by his side. I can see his big, bony hands snaking under the crust of clay, digging deep to pull out root and clump. He shakes each handful vigorously, like a terrier killing a rat, before firing them into the furrow where they will wither and die in the sun.

Weeds are his enemy. He knows each one by its Irish name as passed down to him by his father and his father's father. *Ceathrú caorach, cupóg sráide, blisceán, fearbán, fliodh*. The *ceathrú caorach*, or sheepshank, is tall and easy to pull. He picks it up and flings it in the furrow like a trump card. The wily chickweed, or *fliodh*, requires a different approach. It creeps between the seedlings and fragments at the slightest touch. He plucks it between thumb and forefinger as if he were plucking the down from the breast of a goose. Whenever he comes to the hated dock, or *cupóg sráide*, he gouges into the earth with his calloused fingers to get the tapered end of the root. When he does he grunts with satisfaction, calls it an ugly name, and continues his unyielding attack.

I, on the other hand, never came to terms with weeding. The age-old, relentless and seemingly hopeless war against thistle and thorn was too much for me. I became a deserter. I dreamed of some heavenly place over the road and beyond the hill where I hoped weeds would never grow. One by one the weeders left, and my father grew old in a changed landscape. Cattle grazed where there had been crops and soon the sugar factory in Tuam closed its rusty gates for good.

But while he had life in him, he sharpened the scythe and went into the fields and cut the thistles, and if you watched his stooped frame stumbling towards the evening sun to bring in the cows, you would notice that he could never pass by a nettle growing near a fallen stone without swiping at it with his stick.

And as I crouch here now in the gloaming of my small suburban garden, letting the soil filter through my white hands, I get that old familiar feeling of something lost. In the shadow of the cherry tree I imagine, for a split second, that I see him, hunched over the soil, grappling with it, part of it, part of an ancient battle bounded by nature and nothing else, and I realise that in the span of one short lifetime I have lost what it took centuries to celebrate.

The Turkey Trot

It may seem strange, but talk of turkeys does not remind me of Christmas at all. I see myself cycling down a white dusty country road, past limestone walls and under the dappled canopy of trees in the heat of a bright spring day. My friend and neighbour, Joe, his tousled head thrown back, is cycling beside me, confidently bobbing up and down of the pedals of his mother's high Nelly. We were both about nine years old, but we were entrusted with a very serious mission.

Hanging from the handlebars of my bike was a satchel, and in that satchel was my mother's pride and joy; a big, fat, hen turkey that would, if all went according to plan, produce a nice clutch of chicks that she could fatten for Christmas. The turkey's neck stuck up proudly from a small opening in the top of the bag. Joe's Mammy had given her turkey a pillion passenger's seat in a cardboard box on Joe's carrier, the box all bound with binder-twine. Her turkey's neck, too, was like a periscope in the air. There was a smell of hawthorn in the hedges as we passed two men sowing turnips in a field by the road. They looked up and scratched their heads; two small boys on bicycles, carrying two turkeys.

We were heading for Nohilly's in Cordarra. They had a prize turkey cock. Now you probably get the picture. Our mammy turkeys were going on a kind of honeymoon; a little bit of fun in the sun. You could even sense that they were full of a kind of frenetic anticipation. They gobbled incessantly to each other and fidgeted restlessly within the confines of their respective accommodations. Joe wished he understood turkey language. Even though we were only nine years old, we felt somehow that we were playing some important part in the great process of nature.

But no great mission is without its element of danger. Because I was so small, I had to ride my father's bike with my right foot under the crossbar, so that the bike tilted at a crazy angle to the road. It soon became clear to me that Joe's turkey was travelling first class. Mine was down with the steerage. As we whizzed down the hill past the graveyard, the satchel was swaying precariously and bumping against the wheel of the bicycle.

Then the unthinkable happened. As I swerved to avoid a pothole, the turkey managed to stick its head between the spokes. There was a sudden strumming sound as if from a dull harp and the bicycle came to a sudden halt.

Death must have been instantaneous. There was no blood, but the turkey's neck, when I managed to extricate it, was considerably longer than it had been. The bird looked more like a kind of a hairy swan. There was a mystified look in its eye. Joe Biggins insisted that we continue on to the end of the road. 'We might as well get half the job done, anyway,' he said.

We watched from outside a small corral as his protégée did the turkey trot with her newfound mate. She seemed to be a reluctant lover. I knew that her heart wasn't really in it because she kept running away. I figured that she missed her travelling companion, but Joe said, 'Females are always like that.' He was very wise for a nine-year-old.

When I finally got home, my mother was sad at losing the turkey, but my father took one look at the distorted corpse lying in the yard and burst into an uncontrollable fit of laughter. 'It's a pity it didn't happen on the way home,' he said. 'She would at least have died a happy death!'

Now, every Christmas, when I see the basted bird on the table ready to be devoured, I wonder if there is a chance that she died happy.

Something to Live For

There's a bestselling book by Victor Frankl that tells of the author's harrowing life in a concentration camp during the Second World War. The prisoners spent their days and nights in a state of utter degradation and unimaginable suffering. They were beaten and starved. They seemed to have no hope, nothing in store for them but slave labour, suffering and death in the gas chamber. Nobody knew if this life, for them, would ever end. So, many of them simply ended their lives by running into the electric fence that bounded the camp: a final race towards freedom, in a way.

Frankl, a qualified psychiatrist, found it tremendously difficult to convince the other inmates that they should not give up, that they had a reason to live. Many had lost their families, their homes, their health, their dignity. Apathy was the great enemy. Whenever a prisoner lay down on his wretched bunk and refused to get up, in spite of being beaten and ordered to do so, his friends knew that the end had come for him. He had given up.

There is a memorable episode in Frankl's book where he is asked by a friendly block warden to try and exhort his fellow prisoners to hang on to life. Morale had become particularly low. The harsh, grey, Polish winter was cutting into their skeletal bodies, sharp as a razor.

There was a power failure and the place was dark as the grave. The smoke from the gas ovens hung low over the camp. They knew what it meant.

Dr Frankl used all his skill as a psychiatrist to try and persuade the other prisoners not to give up hope. As they listened in the freezing darkness of the prison hut, Frankl spoke quietly to them. He was one of them. 'Do not let all that you have suffered be in vain. Someone looks down on each of us in times of trouble – a friend, a wife, somebody alive or dead, or a God – and he would not expect us to disappoint him. That which does not kill me makes me stronger.'

Frankl asked some probing questions. A fellow prisoner confessed that he had a first grandchild living in a foreign country whom he had never seen. He was not even sure if the child was alive, but he saw the face of that child in his dreams. The face smiled, and the child stood in a meadow, beckoning. There was a scientist who had written a series of books which still needed to be published. 'It is impossible to replace a person,' Frankl pointed out. 'When you realise this, you know that you have a responsibility to stay alive.'

I suppose we go about our daily lives never pausing to reflect on the fact that our lives make a difference to someone, no matter how hidden that effect might be. Our words have made a difference to someone, our touch, our smile, our tentative pointing out of the way. Our spirit somehow leaves a space.

Last week, in a way, I was reminded of Frankl and his

remarkable story. There was a barber I thought of as my barber. His place was in the city, a small space dwarfed now between two soaring new developments that sought to kill his shop and his ripe old life by drowning it in shadow. He knew me whenever I walked in. He was my philosopher. He would pause sometimes, his twinkling eyes looking at me in the mirror, and make a smiling, seldom sorrowful comment on life. Though he was the last of his generation with nobody left to carry on his trade he never bemoaned the fact. Last Saturday I went for a haircut. The place was boarded up. There was no sign on the window. The red and white pole still leaned precariously over the door. I enquired in several premises until eventually, a Chinese man in a restaurant across the road told me the sad news.

I was angry for my own selfish reasons. I never knew his surname. He had gone without telling me. My life was diminished somehow. But then I thought of his cheerfulness, his record of no regret. I suppose I regretted the fact that I never told him how he made a difference to my life.

Look out for that space you fill. Inhabit it carefully. It will still be there when you are gone.

Sleepers in That Quiet Earth

We go there together, her mother and I, to that suburban cemetery, usually on a Sunday afternoon. It is a wide, flat area, bordered by trees and buildings; the noise of traffic close by. It is a geometric place, plotted and pieced between regular paths, not like the little country graveyard in the west where my mother and father lie, which is all a confusion of winding paths and grassy knolls where you have to have local knowledge and a bit of history to find someone. This is a huge suburban place: it is only size that will defeat you if you fail to find your way.

We walk in familiar directions, as if following streets and side streets, by now accustomed to each turn, past recognisable headstones and epitaphs. Our journey reminds me sometimes of flying over a city at night, imagining the life denoted by each light beneath. We are by now familiar with the names we pass. We note as usual the young and old, but without admitting it to each other, it is the young who set us thinking most. In our minds we see faces: we speculate as to cause and circumstance. Yet, in a strange city way their deaths only concern us in passing, in the way that one house marks the direction, leading to another.

Her plot is off the tarmac and down one section, at a

corner where two gravel paths meet. Her white marble headstone marks the spot. We look for any stain on the marble. We always bring detergent to keep it clean. We cut the grass and replace the flowers, take away the withered, water the growing. We keep focused on the surface. What lies underneath the earth is banished from our thoughts, pressed down resolutely into our own private burial places.

'We must trim that grass at the edge.'

'Next time we'll bring a spade for those weeds close by on the path.'

'We could use that chemical stuff, maybe?'

'No, I think it's better to dig them up.'

There are days when the weighty sense of futility makes us fractious and we work in a kind of numbed detachment, each one silently scorning the work of the other. But together and separately we are faced with our own family name on the white marble, and our child's name always shocks us, no matter how often we come here. Her own name that we gave her, that we called her by, that she answered to, on a stone now, looking back at us. Each time we visit, we strive to give that name life again, to resuscitate it, to infuse it with her laughter and her look. Not a visit goes by but we try to remember something: a word, a look. We look around at the lonely monuments and we fear forgetfulness.

There is, inevitably, a routine in what we do; first the clearing away, then the planting and the watering. The worst time is winter, when the earth is cold and unresponsive. Spring is best, when there is a promise about the sun and a warmth returning to the earth. And because we always finish with a prayer it is important that the sun is out, shining on the white marble and on our backs as we stand with heads bowed. We have a routine of prayers as well. If the truth were to be told we pray not so much with hope or faith but with a kind of a habitual, stony, stubborn defiance.

As I wend my way back by the places of the young and old towards the gate of the world outside I often think of *Wuthering Heights*, the book she read and loved in her last shortened year of school. The closing lines rise and fall with our faltering footsteps: 'I lingered round them, under that benign sky: watched the moths fluttering among the heath and hare-bells; listened to the soft wind breathing through the grass; and wondered how any one could ever imagine unquiet slumbers for the sleepers in that quiet earth.'

The Other Side of Silence

I sat beside a young girl on a bus the other day. She had a musical device plugged into her ear from which a continuous din could be heard clearly, even by the passengers around her. It did not sound in the least like music. All I could hear was a constant, repetitive drumbeat. When the bus lurched round a corner, her earpiece became detached. She became immediately distressed, as if she had suddenly lost some kind of lifeline.

It set me thinking of the nature of sound and the value of silence and the way we have to balance them. Why do people need noise? Are we addicted to noise? Do we no longer need peace and quiet? Could we handle the absence of sound around us? Is there a place where we can go?

My mind returned to a bed under the thatched roof, where, in the dead of night, if you woke up, the silence around you had a kind of a ring to it, a hum of emptiness. And sometimes it might be disturbed only by the swish of wind on the roof outside, a soft sound only, sighing on the senses like a whisper.

There was the silence of an empty church, where, at midday you might turn your head thinking you heard a slipper on the tiles behind you, only to find nobody there. There was the quietness of fields, on a hot June day sitting on a headland when the wind rested for a while and the birds went inexplicably quiet. At a moment like that you felt that the ancestors who had shaped the fields had come back to see that nothing had changed. Do I need to find that silence again?

Maybe there is, for some of us at least, a refuge in noise and clamour. Maybe there is a need for us to have a protective layer between what is around us and what is deep within. Perhaps it is necessary to block out the world, to insulate us from the suffering and the pain that we see but cannot change. Could it be that we cannot dare to confront the starkness of the soul within? I think of the words of George Eliot in *Middlemarch*:

> If we had a keen vision and feeling of all ordinary human life, it would be like hearing the grass grow and the squirrel's heart beat, and we should die of that roar which lies on the other side of silence.

I often think of her words when I wake in the darkest hour of the night, just before light. In that silence, regret and pain and loss of love and all the demons of darkness drop easily into the mind and spread like a drop of ink in a glass of water. This is the hour of isolation, where there is no comfort.

It is then I value birdsong and the sound of human voices.

The Family Tree

'Now I want you all to do a family tree for your homework.'

It was about thirty-five years ago and I was a young teacher teaching in my home place, a small rural school in the west of Ireland. They were a class of nine-year-olds, ready, I believed, to wrestle with the wonderful concept of history. Where did we all come from? How did we begin? Who went before us to hew out the path, to clear the place for our footprint?

The little pool of faces looked up at me, white and expectant out of that shadowy, high-windowed space. The rain drummed on the glass outside and the wind rose and fell mournfully in the empty fireplace. There was a pervasive smell of damp clothes. It was the kind of a day for history.

I had explained at length how our past began before we did, how there was a story to our lives that made each of us at once different and yet in a way the same. We all lived in the same place yet each of us had a unique story to tell as to what and who made us what we are. I had drawn the big tree on the blackboard and pointed, explaining how name branched out into name. 'Here is your father's father. Your mother and father are on these branches. Here you are with your brothers and sisters.

You can write in their names on the leaves if you like.'

I stood at the window while the children gathered their damp coats to go home. The fields towards the dark hills were filling with rain. I thought how this was the place where their history began. In these walled-in spaces their forefathers ploughed and sowed and harvested, married and struggled to survive. Beyond the hills over there was unknown territory for them. Their need and their want were close by. Uncle and aunt, cousin and in-law all a stone's throw away, ramparts in the safe enclosure that surrounded them.

As a child I, too, had listened by the fireside to talk of relations.

'No, the Lees of Curraghmore were no relation to the Lees of Carnakib.'

'Faith then they were! Didn't Thomas Lee marry a daughter of Mary Ellen's?'

Everything was traceable and traced. Nothing was hidden or confused, although some things were hushed.

I wondered now how the children would fare with their homework. I imagined the questions at home, the guarded answers.

The next morning the sun shone slanting through the windows of the classroom, picking out the dancing motes of chalk dust. There was a scent of fresh milk and buttered bread as I walked between the rows of desks surveying the open copybooks of family trees, some rough, some intricate, the stark black and white and the neatly highlighted. Then a blank page stared back at me, above it an upturned apprehensive little face.

'Michael, did you not do your family tree for me?'

'I couldn't, sir.'

'Did you ask anyone to help you, Michael?

'I asked Mammy, sir.'

'And what did she say?

'She told you to mind your own business, sir.'

There was no insolence in the answer, only a quiet mixture of respect and certainty. It was only a slight jolt in the great wheel of learning. His family had inhabited these parts and no other place. They had intermarried and procreated with gusto. They were a formidable force. I had stepped on hallowed ground and I had the good sense to walk on.

I stood at the back of the classroom as the copies were gathered and looked out the window at the countryside between the school and the distant hills. There were trees, too, and in this April sunshine they were donning their summer cover. Some were tall and straight and some were tangled, but they were all beautiful. And they all had roots that were hidden.

Last year I held my grandchild in my arms for the first time. My son lives in Luxembourg. His wife is Swedish. I met her grandfather, a lovely placid man who is a native of Austria. When he was eighteen, he said, he was conscripted into Hitler's army and fought in the Russian front.

I thought as I gazed into my little granddaughter's blue untutored eyes about her growing up and going to school and wrestling with her first concept of history. I thought of her family tree and remembered an old schoolhouse bounded by the hills. The gate of the world has opened wide and the trees are fast-rooted and branching out, hopefully, to the sun.

The Curfew Tolls
the Knell of Parting Day

I went home to visit my mother shortly before she died. She sat by the fire as the evening stretched into night and the old clock on the kitchen wall chimed the tenth hour.

'The curfew tolls the knell of parting day,' she quoted in her frail, lilting voice. Even in the desert of her failing faculties there was an oasis of learning somewhere deep within her mind. Secondary-school education was a luxury that was never available to her, and so, knowing that all the repertoire of her learning was contained in the old national school books, I determined to find, somewhere, a book from which she would have learned. I felt that if I ever found it, it would be a kind of tribute to her, a testament to her spirit and her love of fine words.

I found such a book, covered in dust, in the book-bin of an old country school. It was called *The Fifth Reading Book*, published by Browne and Nolan in 1905. To me it was something sacred, knowing that she would have studied the poems and the lessons within its dark-brown covers. As I reverently opened it, I was transported back to that old, two-roomed country school overlooking Lough Corrib, to a time before independence, a time of poverty of the body and richness of the soul. From its fragile pages her childhood unfolds like the petals of a pressed flower coming to life and 'Fond memory brings the light of other days around me.'

My mother was forever quoting the great poets of English literature, and they are all here in this old primary schoolbook; Milton, Shakespeare, Pope, Tennyson. These old poems were close to her heart. It was from her I learned to love the music and rhythm of spoken verse and the nobility of thought that inspired these imposing lines. When I read 'The Burial of Sir John Moore' I am a child again, huddled by the big kitchen fire with the low moan of the wind in the wide chimney. She is sitting in the wide-armed Windsor chair on the other side of the fire, darning a sock. The clock has just struck ten and I know a cold bed beckons. She looks at me and begins to recite in a tone of lofty sorrow:

> But half of our heavy task was done
> When the clock struck the hour for retiring:
> And we heard the distant and random gun
> That the foe was sullenly firing.
>
> Slowly and sadly we laid him down
> From the field of his fame fresh and gory;
> We carved not a line, and we raised not a
>   stone,
> But we left him alone with his glory.

The standard of English in this book is mesmerising: 'Rosstrevor is built on an acclivity which ascends gracefully from the margin of the water.'

This is English from another age. I find it hard to imagine children nowadays reading sentences like these out of one of the many books that weigh down their schoolbags. But 'the old order changeth, yielding place to new,' as Tennyson says here, 'lest one good custom should corrupt the world'.

There was, indeed, an old order here, a lesson in every story, a moral in every poem.

'There is no remedy for time misspent, no healing for the waste of idleness,' Aubrey de Vere reminds us.

Scott stirs the soul with love of country:

> Breathes there a man with soul so dead,
> Who never to himself hath said,
> This is my own, my native land.

This is a noble patriotism, with no lust for blood or battle, but a burning pride in one's own birthplace.

The old Celtic mythologies are celebrated here by Thomas Moore, my mother's favourite. With my eyes scanning the must-scented pages of her old schoolbook, his words ring out in her voice:

> Silent, oh Moyle, be the roar of thy water,
> Break not, ye breezes, your chain of repose,

While, murmuring mournfully, Lir's lonely
        daughter
Tells to the night-star her tale of woes.

And it was clear that wisdom, too, was something
treasured then, love of the pithy proverb, the aphorisms
of trusted truth. Benjamin Franklin's 'Sayings of Poor
Richard' were forever present in these old books,
cherished by my father, who grew up believing that
wisdom was a trait of strength and power. He murmured
these old proverbs through many thankless tasks:

'The used key is always bright,' as Poor
        Richard says.
'When the well is dry they know the worth
        of water,' as Poor Richard says.

As I turn the yellowed leaves of this old schoolbook
and the years fly away behind me, I become a learner in
another world, a simple world, short in knowledge but
rich in values. Once again I am back again in the flagged
yard of that old two-roomed school in Claran and from
inside the high windows I can hear, drifting out to me
in the still air, the voices of innocence intoning in singsong unison the Latin roots from the end of the *Fifth
Reading Book*:

'*Aedes*,' a house, and '*facio*,' I make, as in
'edifice'.

'*Ager*', a field, and '*colo*', I plough, as in
    'agriculture'.
'*Animus*', the mind, and '*magnus*', great, as in
    'magnanimity'.

And the cold wind of time blows up from the lake, scattering the leaves of the old schoolbook and reminding me that we have lost these old words and their meaning, and with my back to the west wind I wander, lost, down the white winding road, past the neglected fields, past the old thatched house, to a slanting headstone in the shelter of a limestone wall. And the last poem from this old relic of a book echoes round me, chanted by a child from a vanished generation:

> Let not Ambition mock their useful toil,
> Their homely joys and destiny obscure;
> Nor Grandeur hear with a disdainful smile
> The short and simple annals of the poor.
> Far from the madding crowd's ignoble strife
> Their sober wishes never learned to stray;
> Along the cool sequestered vale of life
> They kept the noiseless tenor of their way.

The Silver Dollar

I managed to lift the big, heavy suitcase into the boot of the Morris Cowley even though I was only a puny ten years old. I was so excited I could have lifted the car itself. I was going to serve Mass at the Stations in Cloonkeely, the biggest village in the parish. There was always a collection for the priest and the altar boy at the Stations, so it was a kind of testimonial, a pay-off for all the early morning Masses and the hassle of learning the Latin responses.

Earlier that morning, under the tetchy supervision of Canon Morgan, the big suitcase had been packed with altar stone and wine bottle, golden chalice and braided chasuble, Mass book and bell and blessed candles. I had already put my own little brown case, with its starched and ironed surplice and long black soutane, into the back seat.

I stood outside the church in the misty morning and waited for the canon and the curate to appear from the sacristy. I felt really good. Across the road the grey hulk of Claran school loomed out of the fog. No school for me this morning. No worries about what kind of a mood Mrs O'Hanrahan was in. With any luck I would miss the dictation that we were supposed to have learned. No mental arithmetic either. I could do my own. Thirteen houses in Cloonkeely; probably eight at a shilling and five at sixpence. If it cost nine pence to get in, how many times could I go to the pictures for ten and six? That was the kind of mental arithmetic I liked. The door of the sacristy opened before I could work out the answer, and the two priests emerged.

Father Hegarty, the curate, was tall and thin, with jet-black hair sleeked back straight from his forehead. He was only just out of the seminary and he looked pale and undernourished. Canon Morgan was small and fat and grey-haired, with a round, red face. He looked as if he was always worried about something. He had been in the parish a long time. He knew everybody's history, and he expected people to jump to his command.

'Is everything in?' he asked sternly.

'Yes, Canon,' I replied, hoping that nothing had been overlooked. I would be the one to blame if something was missing.

Soon we were gliding down country lanes, where the grass grew between the wheel tracks and the longer tendrils of briar and hazel whipped off the windscreen. The leather upholstery was smooth against the backs of my knees and there was a faint smell of incense mingled with the stronger scent of pipe tobacco.

'Where are we off to today?' Father Hegarty asked, rubbing his hands and turning to wink at me. I liked him. He played football with us sometimes in the schoolyard.

'John Fahy's, down by the lake,' the canon replied in his gruff voice. 'He's the one who paid the big price for the Kinsella's place. And he still has his Confirmation money to spend!'

'I think I know him,' the curate said. 'He never married, did he?'

'Nobody would have a dowry good enough for that boyo. His sister Nora is home from America now. They say she's really loaded.'

'Is she the one that married the...?'

'You're very well up, for a blow-in,' the canon interrupted. 'She never came home, not even once in forty years, until now.'

'Would you blame her?' Father Hegarty asked, half under his breath.

The canon gave no answer, but he did not seem too happy with that question. He just wiped the condensation off the windscreen and grunted.

I did not understand the conversation at all. It was the first time in my life I had heard a woman described as 'loaded'. I imagined a huge, fat woman, as big as a donkey maybe, with two creels of turf on her back.

I slipped my hand into the leather loop that hung from above the window of the car, bracing myself against the turns and twists of the road and feeling my stomach left behind in mid-air whenever we shot over a little hill.

We made a sharp turn up an even narrower lane that twisted viciously for half a mile and suddenly came to what looked like a clearing in the hazel wood. The house was a low, thatched, whitewashed cottage, its window frames and door newly painted in bright red. There was a gravel path leading from the little garden gate down to a pier which jutted out into the brooding lake. Small groups of men were gathered round the door, dressed in their Sunday clothes, and they doffed their caps as we passed in with the suitcases.

Inside, a bright ash fire crackled on the hearth and the smell of fresh paint and wood smoke filled the warm kitchen. The big kitchen table had already been mounted on two chairs and covered in a crisp, white linen cloth to make a high altar.

Each of the two priests went into a room on either side of the kitchen to hear Confessions. I proceeded to unpack the altar stone and candles and everything else in the order the canon wanted, all under the watchful eye of the women who were seated around the walls. Opening my own little case and donning the starched surplice, I felt as important as a doctor who had come to save a dying man, while the household looked on in awe. It was not the same as in the church. Here, in the confined space of the small kitchen, with people so close, the silence was compacted and condensed; there was no room for mistakes. Still, I managed a sweeping glance around the room to see if I could spot the fat woman, but there was no sign of anyone who might fit the description.

The men filed in and the Mass began. I kept my concentration, though the stone floor was hard on my knees. The Latin responses never bothered me. At last it was over and I could fix my attention on the money. The

man of the house, as was the custom, put out two chairs
on the floor in front of the altar and Canon Morgan took
out his red, dog-eared passbook.

'John Lee, Senior,' the canon intoned, standing
behind the altar and looking out at the people over the
top of his spectacles. A stooped, bony old man shuffled
forward and dropped a pound note on the priest's chair
and a shilling on mine.

'John Lee, Senior, one pound,' the curate called from
his position beside the chair. The canon marked it down.

'William Murphy.'

A short, stocky man with a weatherbeaten face moved
quickly forward, leading with his left shoulder, his head
bowed and his eyes on the floor as if he was walking
against a strong wind. Without once looking up, he
slapped a ten-shilling note on the priests' chair as if it
were the ace of trumps. He then threw sixpence on my
chair before veering away and shouldering his way back
into the crowd of men at the back door.

Each householder in turn came forward when his
name was called and placed money on the chairs. Some
paid a pound and some a ten-shilling note, and a shilling
or sixpence to the clerk.

The priest was closing his notebook when she spoke
from the parlour door – a loud, clear voice from another
world outside the one we knew. 'You don't have my
name on your books, Father, but I guess I'd like to make
a contribution.' The voice cut into the cosiness of the
kitchen like a cold blade, and when the silence returned,

it tightened as if to try and heal the wound.

'The name's Nora Leroy.' There was a low murmur from the men at the back door, and the women around the fireplace exchanged darting glances. A tall, stately lady strode forward to the priests' chair. She must have been about sixty years old, with red lipstick, a black feather slanting out of her hat and a dead fox draped around her neck. She tossed a five-pound note on the priests' chair and a big, bright, silver coin rattled on to mine. I was sure it was a half-crown. The woman wore a satisfied look as she made her way back to the parlour door.

When the priest nodded in my direction, I gathered the coins from my chair and found among them a silver dollar, with a picture of an eagle on it and some Latin words that I could not pronounce. I forgot to count the rest of the money; I was so fascinated by the dollar's solid weight and roundness, turning it over and over in my hand.

The American lady joined her brother, the priests and me in the parlour afterwards for the customary breakfast of grapefruit segments, boiled eggs and toast. She was not shy, like the local women were when they talked to the priest. She talked confidently, like a teacher. She told us all about leaving for America in the 1920s when she was only sixteen, and how she could remember her mother and father crying as they stood on the little pier just down from the house and watched her board the steamer for Galway. She never saw them again. She studied to be a nurse, worked night and day, sent home as many dollars as she could.

'My husband was a surgeon in the hospital where I worked. He died last year. He was from Cuba.'

Silence again: a different silence this time, as if that cold steel blade had finally touched a nerve.

You could tell that silence made Nora Leroy uneasy, that it was alien to her somehow. She looked straight at her brother who was busy stirring his tea. She switched her steady gaze back to the canon before she spoke again.

'You know, Father,' she said evenly, 'my mother must have been praying hard for me all these years. There must be about five million people in New York alone, people of all races and creeds, yet out of all those millions, I met the kindest, truest, most loving man in the entire wide world.'

After she had finished speaking, she continued to look him straight in the eye. He lowered his eyes to the crumbs he was playing with on the white cloth and kept nodding his head silently.

On the way home in the car, I asked Father Hegarty what the words on the silver dollar meant.

'"In God We Trust" on the front....that's easy enough. "*E Pluribus Unum*" on the back. That's Latin for "Out of Many, One." Would you like to swap it for a half-crown?' he asked. I knew he was only half-joking. I think he was just trying to make conversation, because the canon was not in a talking mood.

'No thanks, Father,' I said, feeling the comfort of the heavy roundness in my palm. 'I want to keep it.'

I thought of the words of Mrs Leroy at the breakfast table, about her meeting someone special out of many. '*E Pluribus Unum.*'

I kind of liked her. I felt she had given me a sort of history of her life, in a silver coin. And I was looking forward to searching for Cuba in the atlas when I got back to school.

The Spaces Between Songs

My grandson showed me his latest toy the other day. It's called an MP3 player. Stores up to three hundred songs, he tells me. I find that incredible.

It must be hard for young people to imagine what it was like for their counterparts in the late 1950s (namely, my generation) who could not record a song at all. We could buy pre-recorded discs, and play them on a gramophone, if we had one. That was it.

I remember the first tape-recorder I ever saw. It belonged to a friend of ours who worked in the local town and bought it at an auction. It had two spinning spools of brown magnetic tape and switches as big as the knobs on the dresser. He fancied himself as a singer, played the guitar and held regular music sessions in his house. We would all gather there for a session.

Up to then, our musical sessions were very impromptu, you might say. There was lots of spontaneous craic, and laughter and stories that were not always polite. The man with the tape-machine tried to change all that. He wanted his music recorded for posterity. He failed miserably. The rest of us just wanted a laugh, I suppose, and there was something magical about hearing a recording of rude noises and uncontrollable laughter. Wouldn't I love to hear an unedited version of those carefree hours now!

When my own children were teenagers the cassette recorder was the great innovation for them. You could record songs and music off the radio. Make your own compilation, write the title on the stick-on labels, break the seal and make them permanently yours, impossible to tape over, your own personal collection.

I have a number of cassettes like these that are very special. They were not made by me, but by someone we loved who is no longer here. They are old pop songs that I like. And they comfort me when I'm feeling down. But most of all, I find myself listening even more intently to the intervals between tracks. In those spaces I sometimes believe that I can hear a breath drawn, or a faint whisper. And the deceptive silence between the final chord of one track and the opening of another becomes a space where memory and imagination coalesce. I am, for a fleeting magic moment, in another place and another time.

Modern perfection of sound reproduction is marvellous. But it's the spaces between songs that I really like.

What Will Survive of Us

Even though you may have already seen many of the wonders of Rome your first entrance into the Pantheon is a shock. The awe-inspiring domed interior is the great symbol and synopsis of Rome itself. Its scale and beauty encompass you, and inside this vast vaulted space you feel small and mortal. One hundred and forty feet directly above you is the *oculus*, the round opening at the apex of the roof. Through it you can see nothing but the sky, the only source of light, the pathway to the gods above.

This was indeed the Emperor Hadrian's temple of the gods, built almost two thousand years ago. Many shrines now line its walls, altars to saints and monuments to kings, all yearning, as it were, to that rotunda in the roof, that circled view of heaven, that hope of immortality with white clouds passing and eternal space beyond.

One of the shrines along the wall of the Pantheon is a Madonna sculpted by Lorenzetto, and below it is the tomb of Raphael, one of the greatest artists of all time. He is buried here in the Pantheon at his own request. On the right of Raphael's tomb is a memorial to his fiancée Maria, his patron's niece. But Maria, by all accounts, was not his inspiration or his love. For years he loved another, one they called La Fornarina, the baker's daughter, whose real name was Margherita. He said he could not paint without her being by his side. She was his model and his inspiration and it was his wish that she be buried here in the Pantheon with him, united forever under this rounded ring of heaven. Cruelly, when he died at the age of thirty-seven in 1520 she was not even allowed attend his burial.

But if you visit the Stanza of the Signatura in the Vatican and look carefully at his masterpiece, *The School of Athens*, perhaps you will notice that Raphael has immortalised his love for La Fornarina in a far more endearing way.

In the picture are gathered all the great thinkers of the world, arguing over the nature of Truth. Plato is there, and Aristotle, and Euclid and Diogenes. And on the extreme right is Ptolemy, only it isn't Ptolemy, it is the face of Raphael himself gazing intently outwards towards you, the viewer. In fact, of the sixty or so figures in the massive picture he is the only one looking you in the eye. Or is he? On the far side of the picture there is one other. It is a beautiful dark-haired girl in a white robe. She, too, looks you in the eye. Through your eyes and the eyes of generations past and future the eyes of the artist and the baker's daughter join forever.

And I am reminded of that great poem of Philip Larkin, 'An Arundel Tomb', in which the poet contemplates the figures of an earl and countess sculpted in stone atop a long-neglected tomb. The man is dressed in armour, his sword by his side. Nothing remarkable, you might think, until you notice:

> …with a sharp tender shock,
> His hand withdrawn, holding her hand.

The tomb is worn now, the names of the dead illegible, but through that handclasp they are: 'linked, through lengths and breadths of time'.

As I left Rome behind my abiding memory was not of ruined temples or broken monuments to the dead. Instead I see only two young people looking steadily at me from a painting and inevitably I remember the last line of Larkin's poem: 'What will survive of us is love.'

All the House a Stage

It's not long now since the last of our grown-up children fled the nest. For years the rooms rang loud and long to the sounds of life: babies crying in the night; children learning to play a musical instrument; teenagers staking territory. Then, gradually, almost stealthily, all the echoes of the hectic years subsided into silence. And we, the last to leave the stage, eased into an uneasy peace. After years of tiptoeing, scolding, humouring, listening anxiously for the key to turn in the door at four in the morning – eerie silence. Empty rooms.

And so we felt we had a chance to redecorate, redesign even. We thought of beginnings, before children, the first flush of ownership. Now we could reclaim full tenant's rights for the first time in thirty-five years. We stripped the old and faded wallpaper, took up the worn carpet in the sitting room, installed a new fireplace and got the custom-built kitchen that we had always wanted.

For a short while we languished in a newly-painted house purged of its sounds, its secrets, its old associations. And then our life entered a new and wondrous phase, one we had hardly dared to anticipate. We became grandparents. Two little boys and a girl. Unbounded joy. Before second childhood had a chance to set in we had a chance at second parenthood. With unbridled enthusiasm we bought a cot, a baby's buggy, toys. We had to be ready for when they came to visit.

And when they did, assuming the role of visitor now, our grown-up children made the customary remarks. 'Oh, you put in a new fireplace. That's really nice.' But something in their voices betrayed them; there was a fleeting conflict in the eye. Home is a place for familiarity, for remembering.

But life moves on, and throughout this first and historic coming together of three generations you could almost feel the old house heave a sigh of resignation and turn the other cheek, ready to absorb again the once everyday, once familiar, repeated sounds of life. A baby's laughter, an old lullaby sung low in the evening. A scolding for crayon marks on the wall. There is a big hullabaloo about a knob that's missing from a press in the customised kitchen. Somebody drooled into the remote control of the TV and it doesn't work anymore.

When our children and our grandchildren leave again and the house once more sinks into silence, we survey the sitting room and the stain on the carpet that will never come out. But there is a quiet resignation now. Nobody dares mention redecoration. The house has died and come to life again. There are new echoes in the newly painted rooms. A house is a bit like a theatre, I suppose, an empty, meaningless place without music, or drama, or both. And most of all a theatre needs a full house. And we, who are both audience and players, are looking forward eagerly to the next programme of events.

Poems Mentioned in the Text

p. 107 'Grassland and lowing herds…' from Joseph Campbell's 'Unlaboured Fields'.

p. 108 'The silence of unlaboured fields…' from Joseph Campbell's 'Unlaboured Fields'.

p. 110 Thomas Hood, 'I Remember, I Remember'.

p. 138 'But half of our heavy task was done…' from Charles Wolfe's 'The Burial of Sir John Moore'.

p. 139 'Breathes there a man…' from Sir Walter Scott's 'Love of Country'.
        'Silent, oh Moyle…' from Thomas Moore's 'The Song of Fionnuala'.

p. 141 'Let not Ambition mock…' from Thomas Gray's 'Elegy Written in a Country Churchyard'.